THE WORK OF A MAGISTRATE

For
Dr Roger Hickman
with much gratitude

THE WORK OF A MAGISTRATE

John Greenhill, M.Sc., Barrister

SIXTH EDITION

Shaw & Sons

Published by
Shaw & Sons Limited
Shaway House
21 Bourne Park
Bourne Road
Crayford
Kent DA1 4BZ

First Published .... January 1964
Second Edition .... July 1969
Third Edition .... April 1975
Fourth Edition .... September 1980
Fifth Edition .... January 1994
Reprinted .... June 1997
Sixth Edition .... May 2002

ISBN 0 7219 0563 3

A CIP catalogue record for this book is available from the British Library

Printed in Great Britain by
MPG Books Limited, Bodmin

SUMMARY OF CONTENTS

I WILL WELL AND TRULY SERVE HER MAJESTY QUEEN ELIZABETH THE SECOND IN THE OFFICE OF JUSTICE OF THE PEACE AND I WILL DO RIGHT TO ALL MANNER OF PEOPLE AFTER THE LAWS AND USAGES OF THE REALM WITHOUT FEAR OR FAVOUR, AFFECTION OR ILL-WILL

(The undertaking of a Justice of the Peace)

CONTENTS

PREFACE

Many lay magistrates are busy men and women who, in addition to their court sittings, have little time for study. Few of them have been in a courtroom before being appointed as magistrates. Much is now done by means of training to prepare them for their new responsibilities but the judicial role they undertake is never an easy one. The rules of evidence are not, initially, easy to understand and much has to be learned and understood about the procedures of the Magistrates' Courts. What magistrates are told in training sessions may seem widely removed from the reality of the courtroom and, at times, the roles of the various people in the courtroom may appear incomprehensible.

This book is intended as an initial guide for potential and newly appointed magistrates to many aspects of the work that magistrates are called upon to undertake. The role of the magistrate is not one that can be performed in isolation. Only if the people in the courtroom, be they legal adviser, prosecution or defence advocates, properly play their parts can the magistrates fulfil their task to do justice as they see it – which is the purpose and function of the Bench. It is necessary for magistrates to understand the role of the justices' clerk and legal advisers and the purposes of, and restrictions on, the advocates who appear before them. Equally, an advocate cannot be effective if he is ignorant of the duties and responsibilities of the Bench.

Much is required of magistrates in terms of court sittings and other matters such as Bench meetings and committee meetings and there is an on-going programme of training throughout the magistrates' time on the Bench. It is important for magistrates to remember that nobody is forced to become a magistrate and that their functions and responsibilities are often carried out – as in many other spheres in life – in detriment to other matters. The amount of time involved can be considerable.

The Lord Chancellor requires a magistrate to sit for a minimum of 26 half-days each year. In some court areas, however, it is the practice for magistrates to sit for full days. The Lord Chancellor would hope that magistrates will sit on more than the minimum number of occasions and envisages that they will sit somewhere in the region of 35 half-days. The duties and times of sittings are settled by or on behalf of the justices' clerk and rotas of sittings are published. In due course, subject to having the time to spare and sufficient experience on the Bench, a magistrate may volunteer or be invited to sit additionally in the Youth Court, the Family Proceedings Court or as a member of the licensing committee and the betting and gaming committee. All of these extra matters will involve a substantial additional commitment - one which a magistrate must be certain he is able to give.

There is far more to the work of a magistrate than this introduction can convey. However, for all the books and texts on magistrates, their courts and law and procedure, the foremost source of advice and guidance for a magistrate is that of the justices' clerk and the court's legal advisers.

Any judicial appointment puts a person apart from his peers and can make him the target of blandishments and flattery. A magistrate needs to be aware of this both on and off the Bench.

The police are represented in a Magistrates' Court more often than any other body of people. The prosecutor in criminal proceedings in the vast majority of cases is an employee of the Crown Prosecution Service. For those reasons, any privileges or favours offered by either body should be refused and there should be a reluctance to accept either official or unofficial individual or collective invitations to hospitality and entertainment. Certainly, a magistrate should never privately nor informally discuss with a police officer or the Crown prosecutor anything connected with his office. The public's belief in the independence and impartiality of the magistracy must always be maintained.

A magistrate must never allow expediency, personal interest or embarrassment to persuade him into doing something against the dictates of his conscience. Unless a magistrate is confident that his approach to a particular trial will be detached and he is unafraid of the consequences to himself, the magistrate should decline to sit in that case.

Every case needs to be tried with a magistrate's common sense. The public have put their trust in the magistracy, looking to the magistracy to do what they have avowed to do in the words of the judicial oath. To be so trusted is an honour. To accept that honour is to undertake a heavy obligation to the public.

Readers will note that magistrates (as well as defendants, witnesses, etc.) are referred to in the male gender. This is done purely for convenience and is not intended to detract in any way from the status of female magistrates. I am not alone in this practice; it is also adopted by the draftsmen of Acts of Parliament, no doubt because the English language has no single pronoun which applies to people of both sexes.

John Greenhill

INTRODUCTION

The English and Welsh legal system is fortunate to have as magistrates men and women of diverse occupations, background and culture. The vast majority of Magistrates' Courts are presided over by lay magistrates or, as they are sometimes referred to, Justices of the Peace. The other judicial officers who sit in Magistrates' Courts are District Judges who, until recent times, were called Stipendiary Magistrates. They are legally qualified, full-time and paid. Both on and off the Bench, the magistracy as a whole is often judged by the behaviour of each individual magistrate in his public, business or social environment. Honesty and dignity are respected; pomposity should never be mistaken for dignity.

Magistrates are called upon:

(1) To try criminal and civil cases sitting in a public and open courtroom, and pass sentence on offenders who plead guilty or who are found guilty after a trial.

(2) In court and elsewhere to undertake various legal and administrative responsibilities including the control of the sale of alcohol, the licensing of betting shops and the enforcement of court orders, such as payment of fines.

(3) To undertake tasks for members of the public such as the signature of documents, the taking of oaths and the granting of summonses.

(4) To consider the granting of warrants for the arrest of alleged offenders and the search of premises for stolen goods, drugs and a host of other matters.

A crime and a civil wrong both involve the doing of something forbidden by the law or the failure to do something required by the law.

A crime is an act or an omission of such a nature as to require:

(a) the state to intervene for the good order of society; and

(b) the punishment of the offender.

A civil wrong is an act or omission:

(a) that causes another person an actual or notional suffering; or

(b) in respect of which the law entitles another party to a remedy other than the payment of money.

The same act or omission may give rise to both a criminal prosecution and a civil action. A motorist, for example, who drives a motor vehicle without due care and attention, has an accident and injures a pedestrian, may be prosecuted for any criminal offence arising out of the manner of his driving and also by the pedestrian in a civil action for damages in the County Court or the High Court.

Chapter 1

THE HISTORY OF MAGISTRATES AND HOW THEY ARE APPOINTED

The office of Justice of the Peace was first mentioned in statute in 1361.

The fourteenth century was one of the most troubled yet socially formative periods of history. The Black Death struck down the mighty and the unimportant, depopulating large tracts of the country. Soldiers discharged from the wars returned to find the social structure that they had known slowly disintegrating and hastened that disintegration by robbing and looting. Those feudal lords who survived the plague and could, perhaps, have maintained order either added to the chaos by quarrelling amongst themselves or abandoned their domestic responsibilities to fight abroad.

Edward III, faced with a country on the verge of anarchy, required a body of men who were loyal to and prepared to take orders directly from the Crown, and by the statute of 1361 had it ordered that "... in every County of England there shall be assigned for the keeping of the peace one Lord and with him three or four of the most worthy in the County". This gave rise to the office of Justice of the Peace.

From the outset the justices were laden with many and varied duties and, in particular, were required to hunt down, apprehend and judge those who broke the peace within their particular county.

The Tudor sovereigns, desirous of increasing and strengthening their own authority and that of their governments, found the local Justices of the Peace most useful agents. Each sovereign added more and more to the justices' responsibilities and, by the reign of Elizabeth I, they included the raising and distribution of Poor Relief, ensuring that roads were kept in proper repair, fixing the prices of various commodities and wages, mustering local troops for the sovereign, enforcing the rules of good husbandry, and dealing with those who had the temerity to wear articles of clothing that were not fitting for their station in life.

A justice's task was therefore difficult and unpleasant. He was, as now, an ordinary, though worthy, member of the community who had to live and contend with his neighbours. Yet he was the government's agent and the sovereign's wrath was visited on him if he failed to persuade his neighbours to comply with the government's often unpopular demands. A justice's neighbours were, however, next door, while the government was far away in London and, albeit unwillingly, the justices often found themselves standing between the ordinary man and unpopular and improper government demands and decisions. This independence has been handed on from generation to generation and even today, if not abused, is a protection of our freedoms.

From Tudor days until the Industrial Revolution of the late eighteenth and nineteenth centuries, the local justices continued to dispense justice and administer the county. Gradually, the office became the prerogative of one class, the squire in the country and the successful merchant in the towns; men who were arrogantly independent of instruction from their superiors and the murmurings of those below and administered their particular areas with a confidence that made for peace, if not equity.

The Industrial Revolution shattered a social structure that had taken years to build up. It broke ties that held manual workers in small, well-knit and easily controlled communities, and drew the population into ill-prepared towns. It put wealth into the hands of men who, unlike the squire (and to a lesser degree the merchant), could afford to treat employees as though they were inhuman parts of machines. Money, rather than land and commodities became important. Labour was cheap. Local public administration collapsed.

Those who had been local justices either were not available or refused to act in these new and growing towns, with the result that the office became filled by men who were attracted less by its honour than the financial and other advantages that its holder could gain.

Although the rural justices as a whole continued to be men of integrity, many of their urban brothers, particularly those in London and the other large cities, were openly dishonest. So great and numerous became the scandals and abuses that finally only those honest men who had the courage to do so would risk social ostracism by accepting office; fortunately, there were some such men.

It was the combining of administrative authority and judicial responsibility in one man that made the opportunities to be dishonest so temptingly possible. As the prevailing system of local government was generally inefficient, the bulk of the justices' administrative authority was transferred to county and borough councils, leaving the local justices to concentrate on their judicial role.

The appointment of Justices of the Peace is made by the Lord Chancellor or, in certain areas, the Chancellor of the Duchy of Lancaster, on behalf of the sovereign. The Lord Chancellor's concern is to appoint sufficient justices to deal with the workload and to ensure, so far as is practicable, that local Benches comprise a representative cross-section of the community. The aim is to achieve a reasonable balance of gender, ages, political views, ethnic origins, background and occupations.

To assist in the selection process, an advisory committee exists in each "commission area". That committee or, more usually, a sub-committee or panel, will interview candidates for the Bench and make recommendations for appointment to the Lord Chancellor, who is responsible for making the final decision. These committees and their workings used to be shrouded in some secrecy but this is no longer the case and in most areas the names of committee members are made public.

Anyone may apply to become a Justice of the Peace, or may nominate someone else. An application form may be obtained from the clerk to the advisory committee, whose name and address will be obtainable from the local Magistrates' Court. The applicant is asked to submit the names of two referees.

Amongst other things, the advisory committee is looking for

what is sometimes termed a "judicial attitude"; basically this means ordinary sound common sense and an ability to look at issues objectively and to come to reasoned decisions, plus personal integrity, with a good knowledge of people, the court area and the local community.

There are approximately 30,000 magistrates in England and Wales. Although great strides have been made in broadening the membership of Benches, it is still difficult to recruit certain types of people, particularly manual workers and younger people who are building their careers. However, magistrates do now come from a wider range of occupations and backgrounds.

Many magistrates belong to the Magistrates' Association, a national body which, among other things, makes representations on behalf of magistrates to government when new legislation is under consideration. The Association is also consulted by the Lord Chancellor's Department and other government departments. The Association produces "guidelines" on sentencing to assist magistrates in their deliberations and publishes a monthly journal.

To be appointed to sit in judgment of other people is a great responsibility and a humbling one. So long as magistrates approach their duties in that knowledge and spirit, the courts and society are well served.

Chapter 2

COURTS CONCERNED WITH THE WORK OF MAGISTRATES' COURTS

Magistrates are guided by, and must have regard to, the decisions of superior courts. Those courts are:

The Crown Court

This is the court to which Magistrates' Courts commit for trial persons who are accused of serious crimes, to be dealt with as soon as possible in respect of alleged offences of murder, robbery, rape and other serious offences. The Magistrates' Court may also send an offender to the Crown Court for sentence in prescribed circumstances if the magistrates feel that their powers of sentence are insufficient.

A trial in a Crown Court is by jury and is presided over by a High Court Judge, a Circuit Judge or a part-time judge known as a Recorder, or an Assistant Recorder. The High Court Judge usually deals with the very serious crimes such as murder, complex fraud cases and serious assaults or rape. The Circuit Judges and the Recorders deal with all other cases.

The Crown Court is also an appeal court against decisions of Magistrates' Courts. A person convicted of an offence by a Magistrates' Court may appeal against the conviction and/or sentence. An appeal against conviction takes the form of a new trial in the Crown Court. If an appeal against sentence is unsuccessful, the court may confirm the sentence of the Magistrates' Court or pass some other sentence which would have been within the powers of the Magistrates' Court – including a sentence which is heavier or more severe than the one passed by the Magistrates' Court.

An appeal is presided over by a Circuit Judge or, occasionally, a Recorder but in each case with two magistrates.

After two or three years' service, a magistrate will be invited to sit from time to time in the Crown Court with other justices and Crown Court judges.

The Administrative Court of the High Court

This court, formerly known as the Divisional Court of the Queen's Bench Division, acts as an appeal court on questions of law or procedure from the Magistrates' Court, over which it exercises a supervisory role.

The Family Division of the High Court

This court exercises a similar role to the Administrative Court but in family matters only.

In prescribed circumstances, appeals from the Administrative Court of the Family Division and the Crown Court go to the Court of Appeal, either to its Civil or Criminal Division, and appeals from the Court of Appeal may go the House of Lords.

Chapter 3

THE MAGISTRATE AND HUMAN RIGHTS

Human Rights Act 1998

The European Convention on Human Rights was incorporated into the law of this country on the implementation of the Human Rights Act 1998 and sets out matters concerning the rights of individuals to which the courts must have regard and uphold throughout the practices and procedures they operate.

The Convention comprises of a number of "Articles" which set out what are to be regarded as the minimum standards for the protection of the rights which they establish. Further rights are contained in Protocols which are, in effect, supplements to the Articles to represent what are the minimum standards in human rights.

The Human Rights Act 1998 does not create new offences but by the Articles and Protocols sets out the matters which now affect the application of the existing law, practice and procedures and the exercise of those matters in any way compatible with the Convention.

The Articles contain absolute, limited and qualified rights.

Absolute rights: these rights can never be departed from or restricted.

Limited rights: these are rights that may be limited only to the extent provided for by the Convention itself.

Qualified rights: these are rights, the effect of which the Convention itself allows to be qualified or restricted in prescribed circumstances and conditions.

The Articles of immediate concern to the courts are:

Article 6: The right to a fair trial

"(1) In the determination of his civil rights and obligations or of any criminal charge against him, everyone is entitled to a fair and public hearing within a reasonable time by an independent and impartial tribunal established by law.

Judgement shall be pronounced publicly but the press and public may be excluded from all or part of the trial in the interest of morals, public order or national security in a democratic society, where the interests of juveniles or the protection of the private life of the parties so require, or to the extent strictly necessary in the opinion of the court in special circumstances where publicity would prejudice the interests of justice.

(2) Everyone charged with a criminal offence shall be presumed innocent until proved guilty according to law.

(3) Everyone charged with a criminal offence has the following minimum rights:

(a) to be informed promptly, in a language which he understands and in detail, of the nature and cause of the accusation against him;

(b) to have adequate time and facilities for the preparation of his defence;

(c) to defend himself in person or through legal assistance of his own choosing, or if he has not sufficient means to pay for legal assistance, to be given it free when the interests of justice so require;

(d) to examine or have examined witnesses against him and to obtain the attendance and examination of witnesses on his behalf under the same conditions as witnesses against him;

(e) to have the free assistance of an interpreter if he cannot understand or speak the language used in court."

Article 6 contains both absolute and limited rights which have a great effect in the conduct of the court's proceedings.

Article 8: Right to respect for private and family life

"(1) Everyone has the right to respect for his private and family life, his home and his correspondence.

(2) There shall be no interference by a public authority with the exercise of this right except such as is in accordance with the law and is necessary in a democratic society in the

interests of national security, public safety or the economic well-being of the country, for the prevention of disorder or crime, for the protection of health or morals, or for the protection of the rights and freedom of others."

Article 8 contains an important qualified right.

Article 14: Prohibition on discrimination

"The enjoyment of the rights and freedoms in the convention shall be secured without discrimination on any ground such as sex, race, colour, language, religion, political or other opinion, national or social origin, association with a national minority, property, birth or other status."

Article 14 does not provide an independent general right to freedom from discrimination – it can only be invoked in relation to the other Convention rights.

Reasons for magistrates' decisions

The Magistrates' Court is a "public authority" and as such has a positive duty to ensure that human rights are upheld. Many of the rights speak for themselves, for example acting impartially, provision of an interpreter free of charge and giving reasons for decisions. It is this latter matter that is, perhaps, the most far-reaching in that, up until the implementation of the Human Rights Act 1998, magistrates were only obliged to give reasons for their decisions in very few situations, such as when withholding bail and committing an offender to prison. Neither were they formerly required to state the facts as found by them in a trial which led to their decision. This was a matter which was the cause of much concern, particularly for a defendant who was found guilty of an offence: the defendant was unaware of the factual basis upon which the court's decision was made, thus making it difficult for him to challenge the decision in a higher court if he was so minded.

Magistrates are now required to give their reasons for all decisions at every stage of the proceedings, including matters such as adjournments. The reasons will vary according to the decision being made, as will the detail of the reasons. Reasons in respect of a verdict in a trial are probably the most detailed of all. Reasons have to be given after the verdict is announced and cannot be deferred; they must include the facts that the magistrates considered as significant in their decision. The reasons, ideally, should include the following matters:

(1) Facts which were not in dispute.

(2) Facts which were in dispute.

(3) Facts which were found proved.

(4) The extent to which the witnesses were believed or disbelieved and the matters on which the magistrates relied in reaching those decisions.

(5) Any cases cited by the prosecution and the defence.

Obviously, reasons will vary from case to case and the court cannot deal with every piece of evidence but they should be of sufficient detail to enable the defendant to know how and why the court came to its verdict. Once the reasons have been finalised, magistrates might find it useful to consider the reasons – and the language used in delivering them – as follows:

(a) would a reasonable person who had been present throughout the proceedings, hearing all the evidence, submissions and representations, be able to understand the reasons and the court's decision;

(b) would that person be able to decide, having heard the reasons, whether to appeal against the court's decision;

(c) above all, would the particular defendant understand the reasons and the decisions.

The reasons should be recorded in writing – preferably when they have been agreed by the magistrates and before the verdict is announced – and should be kept safely until at least the time limits for an appeal have expired.

The decisions of the court may be by majority. Whilst consensus is always desirable, it will not always, for good reason, be possible. In that situation, the chairman does not have a second or casting vote. The fact that a decision is made by majority cannot be announced in the court and, when the magistrates' decision is announced, the magistrates must appear to be united and it should not be noticeable to anyone in the courtroom from facial expressions, other body language, etc. that the decision is by majority. There is no provision in the Magistrates' Court for any dissenting opinions to be given.

Chapter 4

OUT-OF-COURT DUTIES

In addition to the judicial duties undertaken in the courthouse and in the courtroom, a magistrate will be required from time to time to perform other tasks at home. Some of the tasks may be time-consuming but they must be undertaken with great care. Perhaps the most frequent application made to a magistrate at home is that made by the police for a warrant to search premises for a variety of reasons, such as a search for stolen goods, drugs and firearms. In most courthouses there is a specific time at which applications can be made for warrants. Where a search warrant is urgently needed the application may be made at any time the court is open and there is a magistrate on the premises. However, there will be occasions when a magistrate is not present or when a warrant is urgently needed after the court is closed. In such urgent situations, and only in those situations, a magistrate may consider the application for a search warrant at home. Every court will have guidelines, advice and the telephone numbers of legal advisers who can be contacted for advice in the event of an urgent application. A magistrate is always advised not to act without taking advantage of this guidance. Courts will also provide magistrates with the steps that must be followed when hearing such an application, for example administering the oath or affirmation to the police officer, obtaining a written information signed by the officer and details which must be shown in the warrant. (An "information" is the document in which the police officer sets out the details of the application and the reasons for making it.) It cannot be emphasised strongly enough that these applications must be so urgent that they cannot wait for the courthouse to be open and application made there.

Magistrates, together with ministers of religion, doctors, lawyers and others, are considered sufficiently responsible to witness the signing of various documents. Magistrates are also empowered to take statutory declarations and administer oaths. These are all judicial matters and must be dealt with at the courthouse and not at the magistrate's home. All documents in such matters will be seen and be checked by a legal adviser who will guide the magistrate throughout the particular application. The legal adviser will, for example, ensure that the magistrate is empowered to witness a signature and that the magistrate dates the document the day on which it is signed and signs the document in the appropriate place with the postscription of Justice of the Peace.

A magistrate should be alert to requests such as that of signing a passport application. Whilst a magistrate is a possible signatory to a passport application, he may only sign the appropriate document if he has *personal* knowledge of the applicant and over a period of time which may be specified in that document. The popular belief that a magistrate may sign any passport application is an incorrect one.

The giving of advice

Once a person is known to be a magistrate, it is often the situation that friends and other persons consider the magistrate to be an expert in all fields of law and seek advice on innumerable matters. A magistrate might consider it good advice not to respond and instead inform his questioner to consult a solicitor or seek advice from, for example, the Citizens Advice Bureau. It is also advisable not to name a particular solicitor: an unscrupulous individual might otherwise think that for some improper reason the magistrate favours that solicitor. There may always be someone who would try to make capital from anything a magistrate says and does.

Chapter 5

THE JUSTICES' CLERK AND LEGAL ADVISERS

Every Magistrates' Court area has a justices' clerk who, in addition to being the principal legal adviser to the magistrates, has innumerable administrative duties and responsibilities. It is not practicable here to list all of those matters. Besides legal advice, some of the principal duties and responsibilities are:

(1) The collection and enforcement of fines, compensation and costs and disbursement.

(2) The receipt and disbursement of maintenance payments.

(3) The administration, in addition to the (adult) Magistrates' Court, of the Youth Court, Family Panel and the committees of the licensing justices.

The justices' clerk who has administrative responsibility is also the justices' chief executive. Sometimes there is a separate post of justices' chief executive.

It is the justices' clerk who sets the standards for his court(s) and staff and that of his magistrates. Above all, he is the guide and adviser to all the magistrates assigned to his court area. The happiness and efficiency of the court can very much depend on the attitude of the justices' clerk. His task is not an easy one.

Each time a Magistrates' Court sits, there is a legal adviser – formerly known as a clerk – present to assist the court. In view of the burdens on the justices' clerk, it is unlikely that he will sit in court very often, if at all. In any event, with the number of courts that sit each day, he must have a number of legal advisers to take his place in the courtroom. The legal advisers, like the justices' clerk, are either barristers or solicitors, or other suitably qualified persons.

The justices' clerk is responsible for:

(a) the legal advice tendered to the magistrates within his court area;

(b) the performance of any of the functions of his staff acting as a legal adviser;

(c) ensuring that competent advice is available to the magistrates when the justices' clerk is not personally present in court;

(d) the effective delivery of case management and the reduction of unnecessary delay.

The responsibility of the legal adviser is to provide the magistrates with any advice they require properly to perform their functions, whether or not the magistrates have requested that advice, on the following matters:

(i) questions of law, including the European Court of Human Rights jurisprudence and matters set out in the Human Rights Act 1998;

(ii) questions of mixed law and fact;

(iii) matters of practice and procedure;

(iv) the range of penalties available;

(v) any relevant decisions of the superior courts or other guidelines;

(vi) other issues relevant to the matter before the court;

(vii) the appropriate decision-making structure to be applied in any given case.

Where a legal adviser performs any of those functions, he will have the same responsibility as the justices' clerk and, for the purpose of tendering advice to the court, he may consult the justices' clerk before doing so or consult any other person authorised by the justices' clerk for that purpose. If the justices' clerk or the authorised person is called upon to give any advice directly to the court, he should give the parties or their advocates an opportunity of repeating any relevant submissions which may have been made to the court, prior to the advice being given. In addition to advising the magistrates, the legal adviser has the responsibility to assist the court, where appropriate, with the formulation of reasons for their decisions and the recording of those reasons. The justices' clerk or legal adviser must not play any part in making findings of fact but they may assist the court by reminding them of the evidence that has been given in a case, using any of their notes of evidence.

The legal adviser also has a duty to ensure that every case is conducted fairly and may ask questions of witnesses and the parties in order to clarify the evidence and any issues in the case. In advising the magistrates, the justices' clerk or legal adviser, whether or not previously in the courtroom, must ensure that he is aware of the relevant facts and provide the parties with the information necessary to enable them to make any representations they wish as to the advice he intends to give. Importantly, a legal adviser is under a duty to assist unrepresented parties to present their case, but must do so without appearing to become an advocate for the party concerned.

At any time, magistrates are entitled to receive advice to assist them in discharging their responsibilities. If they are in any doubt as to the evidence which has been given in a case, they should seek the aid of their legal adviser, referring to his notes as appropriate. This should ordinarily be done in open court. Where they request their adviser to join them in the retiring room, the request should be made in the presence of the parties in court. Any legal advice given to the magistrates other than in open court should be clearly stated to be provisional and the adviser should subsequently repeat the substance of the advice in open court and give the parties an opportunity to make any representations they wish on that provisional advice. The legal adviser should then state in open court whether the provisional advice is confirmed or, if it is varied, the nature of the variation.

The role of the legal adviser in fine default proceedings or any other proceedings for the enforcement of financial orders, obligations or penalties is to assist the court. He must not act in an adversarial or partisan manner. With the agreement of the magistrates, a legal adviser may ask questions of the defaulter to elicit information which the magistrates will require to make an adjudication, for example to facilitate his or her explanation for the default. A legal adviser may also advise the magistrates as to the options open to them in dealing with the case. It is inappropriate for the legal adviser to set out to establish wilful refusal or neglect or any other type of culpable behaviour for non-payment of a financial penalty, to offer an opinion on the facts, or to urge a particular course of action upon the magistrates. The duty of impartiality is the paramount consideration for the legal adviser at all times.

The magistrate's duty

A magistrate must never abdicate to a legal adviser his responsibility for making a decision. All magistrates are encouraged to seek their advisers' advice on questions of law and procedure. The court, when retiring to consider matters arising during the course of proceedings, should never ask the adviser to retire with them as a matter of course. They should call for the adviser as and when required and, of course, the adviser is under a duty to give advice even if it has not been sought. In giving advice on sentencing guidelines, it is appropriate for the adviser to inform the court of the penalties imposed by other courts in similar offences so that there may be an element of uniformity in sentence. Magistrates must never ask the adviser for opinions of witnesses' evidence or the veracity of witnesses; nor an opinion whether the defendant is guilty or not guilty; nor what the actual sentence on an offender should be.

Chapter 6

THE MAGISTRATE IN COURT

None of a magistrate's duties is more important than those which are undertaken in public in open court.

Magistrates are required to solve complex legal problems, differentiate between people of truth and perjurers and ensure that the business of their courts is conducted in an orderly manner. All this they are required to do with limited legal knowledge, sometimes without the assistance of competent advocates, but with the sound guidance of their legal adviser.

A magistrate needs to:

(a) approach each case with an open and unprejudiced mind and remain undecided until all the evidence, submissions and speeches have been heard;

(b) be emotionally unaffected by the behaviour of the defendant and witnesses;

(c) be courteous to those taking part in the trial and listen to all explanations and arguments with attention and patience;

(d) ask questions to clarify a matter only;

(e) try each case only on the evidence presented in court; and

(f) having listened to and carefully considered the evidence, the advocates' speeches, the legal adviser's advice and the opinions of the other magistrates, make the required decision with fearless independence.

Above all, a magistrate must be, and appear to be, fair and impartial.

The magistrate and prejudice

All of us are affected to some degree by prejudice as a result of our daily lives outside the court setting. Sometimes we may be unaware of the existence of those prejudices, yet they are discerned by others. A magistrate, in particular, must not be influenced by prejudice. When trying a case the magistrate is not concerned with morality, charity or sympathy; it is the legal and not the moral issue that must be decided.

A magistrate's open mind

To be the first to tell a tale and to be the first to "get in a story" is often seen to be an advantage, and it is easier to appear truthful when making an allegation than when denying one. However, a defendant must wait until those who accuse him have told their story to the court before he is able to start making his denials or give his version of the incident.

A magistrate must, therefore, guard against forming an opinion until all the evidence has been heard.

Rightly or wrongly, the criminal justice process is based on the questioning of parties and witnesses in a public court as the best means of arriving at the truth.

A magistrate cannot always guarantee that his verdict is the correct one. Therefore, he should not hold it against, nor additionally punish, a defendant whose unsuccessful defence has entailed the vehement questioning and contradiction of a prosecutor's witness. Nor should a defendant be punished for any incompetence of his advocate.

Legal knowledge

Our laws are based on the customs of the land (or, to use a more formal phrase, the "Common Law") and Acts of Parliament (also called statutes) as interpreted by judges. Often when Parliament passes an Act its meaning is questioned and requires interpretation by the courts. Once a judge of a higher court has interpreted a statute or given his opinion as to what is the law, judges of the same rank must heed his interpretation or opinion whilst lower courts are bound by it.

Hardly a year goes by without an Act being passed that affects procedure or sentences. Thus, for practical purposes, the law alters daily and no layman can hope to remain up to date in his legal knowledge; indeed, the law is so complex now that professional lawyers are tending to specialise in only one or two branches of it.

Although magistrates are not required to be learned in the law, there may be a tendency on the part of some magistrates to assume that they "know" the law. But a judgment based on imperfect or out-dated information will invariably be wrong; every trial should be started without any preconceived notions as to what is the law.

Magistrates will, of course, wish at all times to uphold the dignity of their office but neither they nor their office lose any dignity by admitting in the public court their ignorance of some legal matter. If a magistrate accepts and acts on a legal argument, or what he is told by an advocate or his legal adviser, without fully understanding the argument and its purpose, he is not acting judicially. If he lacks understanding, a magistrate should say so, and seek clarification or advice from the legal adviser.

Legal quotations

The law involved in trials is not always straightforward. Occasionally, the legal issues are complex. Whether, for example, a building is a "factory" may not be as simple and straightforward an issue as it would appear at first sight and it may be one which might well be taken from the Magistrates' Court to the High Court and then to the House of Lords.

A magistrate cannot, therefore, be blamed if he approaches a legal problem with some trepidation. He should do his best to interpret the Act or regulation and relevant previous decisions of the higher courts, and make up his mind without being fearful of an appeal court disagreeing with his decision. So long as a magistrate has made a reasonable and independent decision and sought the advice of the legal adviser, there is no stigma attached to his decision being altered by a higher court.

Prosecuting and defending advocates are under an obligation to tell the Bench of *all* the law involved in a case, whether that law is favourable or adverse to their cause. Of course, once an advocate has told the magistrates of the law (be it an Act of Parliament, regulation or reported case), he may attempt to interpret it in a manner which is favourable to his client.

Usually, advocates do not need to dispute the existence or wording of a statute or case, only its interpretation. Magistrates may, therefore, usually rely on a quotation from one of the many manuals that are available and the best form of advice – that of the legal adviser or justices' clerk.

The decision is, however, the magistrate's, and he must bear in mind the submissions of the two advocates as well as the legal adviser's advice when making it.

Magistrates and their court

Magistrates can concentrate on the evidence and arguments and reach a reasonable decision only if the trial proceeds in an orderly manner. The responsibility for ensuring that a trial proceeds in this way is that of the Bench and of the chairman in particular. If a magistrate wishes to ask a relevant and permissible question, the question should normally be put through the chairman. If the Bench wishes to make a pronouncement, it should be made by the chairman.

In the courtroom, magistrates usually sit as a group of three, one of them taking the chair. Magistrates' Courts are properly constituted when two magistrates sit but problems may arise when only two sit to try a case: they may disagree over the verdict and, in that event, there would have to be another trial with all the attendant re-organisation and cost. On occasions, a single magistrate may sit to deal with specific matters such as adjourning proceedings, committing cases to the Crown Court for trial or granting summonses.

The legal adviser

Each court will have the assistance of a legally qualified person, referred to as a legal adviser. The role of a legal adviser is set out in what is called a Practice Direction issued by the Lord Chief Justice. A court will not be properly constituted without a legal adviser.

Bias

In law, the only restriction on a magistrate sitting on a particular case is when, for the purposes of deciding issues of bail or custody in the process leading to trial, the magistrate has been informed of the defendant's previous convictions.

That is a total bar to the magistrate sitting on the trial. However, there may be other circumstances in which it might not be appropriate for a magistrate to sit. The circumstances will obviously vary from case to case, some of the following being the more serious:

(1) The magistrate knows well a party to the case or a witness.

(2) He is in the remotest way personally interested in or affected by the result of the trial.

(3) He has been approached about the case or has discussed it with another person.

At the outset of a trial, a magistrate will not necessarily know who is to be called as a witness and may not realise he knows a witness until the witness enters court. When that occurs, the magistrate should ask the legal adviser to adjourn the court and, outside the courtroom and apart from the other magistrates, inform the legal adviser of the matter, seeking his advice. Whatever the situation, even if there is the slightest doubt as to whether the magistrate should sit or not, that doubt must be resolved by leaving the Bench and seeking advice from the legal adviser. There may be situations where a magistrate who is a local councillor sits and cases brought by the local authority are in the day's list. The duty there is obvious. Far better that such matters are raised by the magistrate rather than the matters being brought to the magistrate's attention.

Dress

It is appropriate here to mention the matter of dress. Some magistrates might think that they should "dress up" for sitting in court. Others might prefer to "dress down". Whatever view the magistrate holds on the matter of dress, the rule is come to court dressed appropriately for the work that has to be done: items of expensive jewellery, ties and lapel badges and other things which indicate an affiliation to some other body or organisation are not appropriate in the courtroom – as are all matters which could create an impression of bias in the mind of an observer in the courtroom or affront that person's sense of justice.

Chapter 7

ADJOURNMENT, REMAND AND BAIL

Criminal proceedings are started either by the arrest of a defendant or by the laying of an "information" before a magistrate. An information, if it is in writing, sets out the defendant's name, address and other particulars and the details of the alleged offence. If the information is in writing and is substantiated on oath by the person who lays it, a magistrate has the discretion either to issue a warrant for the defendant's arrest or a summons, which is a direction to the defendant to attend the court on the day and at the time specified in the summons.

A warrant for arrest may only be issued if the alleged offence is indictable or is punishable by imprisonment or if the address of the defendant is not sufficiently established for a summons to be served on him. A warrant may be with bail, that is to say that on arrest the defendant may be bailed to attend the court on a date and time specified by the arresting officer, or without bail in which case the defendant is held in custody and must be brought before the court as soon as practicable. If the application is for a summons, the information need not be in writing nor substantiated on oath. Verbal details will suffice. Some offences carry a power of arrest without the need for a warrant. In such a case, the police may grant bail or, if not, bring the defendant before the court as soon as practicable.

Adjournments and remands

It is not always possible for the case against a defendant to proceed on the first occasion the case is before the court and the court will have to adjourn the proceedings to another occasion.

An adjournment may be needed for several reasons, including matters such as the defendant wishing to apply for legal representation; for the prosecution to serve relevant papers on the defendant, such as advance information which is in the form of written statements or a written précis of the prosecution evidence and tape-recorded interviews; for more enquiries on the part of the prosecution; or, if the defendant pleads not guilty to the alleged offence, to a date when the court can try the case and when all witnesses – both prosecution and defence – can attend to give evidence. When considering an application for an adjournment either by the prosecution or the defence, the magistrates should make enquiry to ensure that the application is a proper one and for good reason. From that time onwards, the magistrates are in effect the "case managers", controlling every stage of the proceedings, avoiding delay, time wasting and ensuring that both sides are doing what is required of them expeditiously.

If the court grants a request for an adjournment to a later date, the court has to decide what is to happen to the defendant in the meantime. Depending on the category and type of offence alleged against him, the court may simply inform him of the date and time at which he is to return to court and then allow him the leave the court. In other cases, the court will "remand" the defendant until the next court hearing, either in custody or on bail. (Note: the court "adjourns" proceedings but "remands" the defendant.)

Period of remand

The period of a remand is governed by the stage reached in the proceedings and whether the defendant is convicted or unconvicted of the offence before the court. The maximum periods of remand are:

(1) If on *bail*:

- (a) *before conviction*, eight clear days unless both prosecution and defence consent to a longer period;
- (b) *after conviction*, four weeks for enquiries or reports.

(2) If in *custody*:

- (a) *before conviction*:
    - (i) eight clear days, to a prison establishment;
    - (ii) four weeks if the defendant consents not to be produced to the court week by week;

(iii) up to 28 clear days if the defendant has previously been remanded in custody in the proceedings and the next stage of the proceedings is to proceed on a specified date;

(iv) 28 clear days if the defendant is a serving prisoner and has at least that period still to serve;

(v) until appearance at the Crown Court if the defendant has been sent there or has been committed there for trial.

(b) *after conviction*:

(i) up to three weeks for enquiries or reports;

(ii) until appearance at the Crown Court if committed there for sentence.

The court also has power, if refusing a defendant bail, to commit him to police detention for up to three clear days if the police satisfy the court that there is a need of it for the purposes of enquiring into other offences, including those already before the court.

If there are on-going enquiries in respect of the offence before the court or other offences, the defendant must be brought back before the court on the expiry of the three-day period. Statute sets out the situations in which the court is obliged to remand a defendant and the legal adviser will inform the magistrates of any obligation that would apply to the case with which they are dealing.

Remands in custody or on bail

There is, before conviction, a presumption in favour of bail for every defendant before the court in criminal proceedings. There is no power to remand a defendant in custody unless that presumption is displaced by one or more reasons set out in the Bail Act 1976, save in the case of a defendant who has been charged with or convicted of murder, attempted murder, manslaughter, rape or attempted rape and has previously been convicted of such an offence and, in the case of manslaughter, is sentenced to imprisonment. Such a defendant must be remanded in custody. To grant a defendant bail means that he is allowed his freedom and is under an obligation to attend the court on the date and at the time appointed for the next hearing.

If the offence or one of the offences with which the defendant has been charged is *punishable with imprisonment*, the court need not grant him bail if it is satisfied that:

(a) the offence is an indictable or either-way offence and it appears that he was on bail in criminal proceedings on the date of the offence; or

(b) if released on bail, with or without conditions, there are substantial grounds for believing that he would:

(i) fail to surrender to custody; or

(ii) commit an offence while on bail; or

(iii) interfere with witnesses or otherwise obstruct the course of justice, whether in relation to himself or another person; or

(c) he should be in custody for his own protection or, in the case of a juvenile, for his own welfare; or

(d) it has not been possible to obtain sufficient information for the purpose of making a decision as to bail because of insufficient time; or

(e) he is serving a custodial sentence; or

(f) he has been arrested for failing to surrender to custody or for breaching a condition of bail.

In deciding whether or not to grant bail, the court may have regard to the following matters if they appear to be relevant:

(i) the nature and seriousness of the alleged offence;

(ii) the character, antecedents, associations and community ties of the defendant;

(iii) the defendant's record as to fulfilment of conditions under any previous grants of bail;

(iv) the strength of the evidence against the defendant.

If the offence(s) with which the defendant has been charged

are *not imprisonable*, bail may only be refused if it appears to the court that, when previously granted bail in criminal proceedings:

(a) the defendant has failed to surrender; and

(b) in view of that failure it is probable that if released on bail, with or without conditions, he will again fail to surrender to custody.

Unconditional and conditional bail

When bail is granted, it may be with or without conditions specified by the court but conditions may only be imposed if it appears necessary to do so to prevent the occurrence of any of the events for which bail may be refused. The conditions may be:

(1) To provide a surety or sureties to secure the defendant's surrender to the court at the next hearing.

(2) To give a security, either himself or on his behalf, for his surrender.

(3) To comply, before release or after release, with such requirements as appear necessary to the court to secure the purposes of the Bail Act 1976.

In the case of a belief that the defendant will not answer bail, a surety might be an appropriate condition to allay the court's fears. This is, in fact, the only situation where the court may impose a surety condition.

A *surety* is a person who undertakes to guarantee the appearance of the defendant at court on the next occasion he is required to do so, on the pain of forfeiture of a sum of money specified by the court if in fact the defendant does not appear. A *security* is a sum of money specified by the court which must be deposited with the court before the defendant can be released on bail. The requirement for a surety or a security is a pre-release condition. A further example of a pre-release condition is the requirement for a defendant's passport to be delivered up to the police. Examples of post-release conditions are the requirement to reside and sleep at a specified address; to report to a police station on days and at times specified by the court; and not to contact directly or indirectly any person named by the court. If the offence alleged is said to have been committed at night, the court, if granting bail, may consider that a curfew is necessary where the defendant is required to be indoors between the hours specified by the court.

If the court fears an interference with witnesses or the obstruction of the course of justice, it may consider imposing a condition that the defendant should not contact directly or indirectly any witness it specifies, which may include an alleged victim.

The defendant who may fail to surrender

The number of defendants who do not answer their bail is small. When the defendant has a home, is living with his family, or is in employment, he may well consider it not worthwhile to jeopardise those matters by not answering his bail and subsequently being remanded in custody. A lack of a home, a settled job or the likelihood of the defendant going abroad are examples of the factors the court would take into consideration when deciding to grant or refuse bail.

The defendant who commits offences

The previous criminal convictions of a defendant may be a reason for the prosecution objecting to bail, but the mere fact that the defendant has previous convictions is not a good reason for refusing bail: the court must consider the categories of the past offences alongside the alleged offence(s) with which the defendant has been charged, the frequency of offending and the pattern of offending. A defendant who does not have previous convictions cannot be presumed likely to commit offences while on bail. The magistrates should always ask to be told of any previous convictions the defendant may have.

The defendant who obstructs the course of justice

The objection under this heading usually relates to the interference with prosecution witnesses in the sense of persuading or frightening the witnesses into lying or refusing to give evidence or otherwise interfere with the prosecution evidence. It cannot be emphasised enough that, if the court is to refuse bail or impose conditions under any of these three headings, it must be satisfied that there are *substantial grounds for believing* that, if it were to do otherwise, the defendant would fail to surrender, commit offences or obstruct the course of justice.

There is no limit to the variety of conditions that may be imposed when bail is granted, but any condition imposed when bail is granted must be warranted, realistic, workable and practical. Whatever decision the court makes in respect of bail, conditional or unconditional, the refusal of bail or the variation of any conditions of bail previously imposed, the magistrates must announce their decision in open court, the exceptions they find to the right to unconditional bail and the reasons for the decision. Further, the decision, the exceptions and the reasons must be recorded in writing by the legal adviser.

Bail or custody after conviction

If a defendant is convicted of an offence and the court adjourns the proceedings, for example for the preparation of a pre-sentence report, there is not a presumption in favour of bail as there is before conviction. However, the court will still need to consider bail or custody in a manner similar to the pre-conviction situation. The same applies when a defendant is committed to the Crown Court for sentence.

Breach of bail conditions

A defendant who has been granted bail with conditions may be arrested by a police officer if the officer has reasonable grounds for believing that the defendant:

(a) is not likely to surrender to the court on the due date; or

(b) is likely to breach any conditions of his bail; or

(c) has broken any condition.

The defendant will then be brought before a Magistrates' Court and, if the court is satisfied of any of those matters, it may remand the defendant in custody or release him on bail with or without conditions to appear before the court which originally granted him bail, on a specified date.

Failure to answer bail

If a defendant who has been granted bail fails to attend court on the due date at the requisite time, the court may issue a warrant for his arrest and, in prescribed circumstances, the defendant may be charged with the offence of failing to answer to bail.

Procedure on an application for bail

As a defendant is entitled to have unconditional bail unless the court finds an exception to that, the court must consider any application for bail with care. The decision whether or not a defendant should have bail is probably the most difficult of all the decisions magistrates have to make.

A prosecutor who objects to the defendant being released on bail during the period of adjournment to the next hearing must tell the court why he objects, setting out the facts of the alleged offence as the prosecution sees them and identifying those matters which it is considered give rise to one or more exceptions to the right to unconditional bail.

Thereafter, if the defendant is applying for bail, he, or his advocate if he is represented, will put to the court all matters and circumstances which they consider relevant to show there is no basis for the prosecution's assertions, or which will allay any fears as to appearance at court, offending and interference with the course of justice, suggesting matters which could be incorporated as conditions of bail. Thereafter, the court will make its decision. If bail is refused or conditional bail is granted, the court must specify the exceptions to the right of unconditional bail they have applied and the reasons for that. If conditional bail is granted, the conditions may be pre-release, post-release or a combination of both. Where the defendant is unable immediately to fulfil a pre-release condition, for example providing a surety or surrendering his passport, he must remain in custody until the condition is fulfilled, or be produced before the court again within eight clear days, whichever occurs first. In that situation, the court will specify the date for production.

Written copy of bail/custody decisions

Where conditional bail or unconditional bail is granted or the defendant is remanded in custody, he is entitled to a notice in writing of that decision. He is also entitled to a copy of any subsequent decision, including the variation of any conditions of bail.

A defendant has the right to make two applications for bail. If he is remanded in custody after the second application, a further application for bail may only be made if there has been a change in circumstances, for example if the defendant had no fixed address and one has become available, or if a surety is forthcoming. However, the court is required to consider the bail situation on every occasion the defendant appears before the court and consider whether it remains necessary to deny bail and keep the defendant in custody.

The responsibility for granting or refusing bail, and the terms on which bail is granted, is the magistrates' alone. Each application, even when two or more defendants are charged together, must be considered on its own merits and it must always be borne in mind that:

(1) Bail must never be refused in order to punish a defendant: no one may be judicially punished until after he has pleaded guilty to, or has been convicted of, an offence.

(2) Unless a defendant has made an admission of guilt, the truth of which he does not deny, he is innocent until he is found guilty at his trial.

(3) It is difficult for a defendant to prepare his defence when he is in a prison or remand centre.

(4) Bail must never be refused in order to ensure that a defendant is readily available to be interviewed by the police.

Where the defendant is remanded in custody and is not represented by a lawyer, the court must inform him of his right to apply to the High Court or the Crown Court for a review of that decision if he is still seeking bail. In order to make that application, a copy of the written bail/custody record must be given to him.

Prosecution right of appeal against the grant of bail

Where magistrates grant bail to a defendant charged with taking a motor vehicle without authority, aggravated vehicle taking or an offence which is punishable by a term of imprisonment of five years or more, the prosecution may appeal to the Crown Court against the grant of bail, but only if the prosecution made representations before the magistrates that bail should not be granted and the representations were made before bail was granted. The prosecution must be one undertaken by the Crown Prosecution Service or by persons prescribed by the Home Secretary.

Committals to the Crown Court for trial; sending an indictable offence to the Crown Court

In each of these situations, the procedure for objecting to bail and making application for bail is precisely the same as the procedure on adjourning a case in the Magistrates' Court and the court will specify the date on which the defendant is required to attend or be brought before the Crown Court.

Restrictions on magistrates sitting at trial after dealing with bail

If, during the course of a bail application, the magistrates are told that a defendant has previous convictions, those magistrates are prohibited from sitting at the defendant's trial if he pleads not guilty to the offence(s) before the court. Obviously, this restriction is imposed in order to prevent a magistrate's decision being influenced by the fact that the defendant has previous convictions. Magistrates may, of course, have heard in other proceedings that the defendant has previous convictions. That is not a bar to sitting at the trial in other proceedings but, even so, if a magistrate has the slightest doubt as to whether he can try a defendant impartially since he knows of those convictions, it is preferable that he refrains from sitting at the trial.

Chapter 8

JURISDICTION: CLASSES OF OFFENCE AND PROCEDURES

Although approximately 98% of criminal cases are dealt with by Magistrates' Courts, there are some offences which cannot be dealt with by them. Criminal offences are divided into three groups:

(1) Summary offences.

(2) Either-way offences.

(3) Indictable offences.

Summary offences

These comprise the vast majority of offences which are dealt with in Magistrates' Courts and can only be dealt with by those courts. Examples are road traffic offences, such as driving without due care and attention, no insurance, defective tyres; common assault; television licence evasion and vehicle excise licence evasion.

Either-way offences

These are so called because they may be tried in either the Crown Court or the Magistrates' Court. Examples are theft, burglary, assault causing bodily harm, obtaining property by deception and certain public order offences.

Indictable offences

These offences cannot be tried by Magistrates' Courts and have to be committed to the Crown Court for trial. They include robbery, grievous bodily harm, murder, rape and conspiracy to commit certain offences.

Every criminal offence consists of different "ingredients", all of which have to be proved beyond reasonable doubt by the prosecution for there to be a conviction of the person accused of that offence. By way of illustration, the following offences are shown with their ingredients:

Theft consists of:

an appropriation or taking;
of property
belonging to another
dishonestly
with an intention permanently
to deprive the owner of the property.

Burglary consists of:

entering a building or part of a building
as a trespasser
with intent to steal or commit other specified offences therein or
actually stealing property or committing other specified offences therein.

Robbery consists of:

stealing property
from a person
and, at the same time and in order to steal or attempt to steal, using or threatening violence on that person.

There are many offences – notably most road traffic offences – which are "absolute" offences not requiring any mental or "guilty mind" element. For example, if a motorist drives a motor vehicle without the requisite insurance cover, his reason for doing that is of no consequence to the offence itself and he is guilty of it. If a provisional licence holder drives a motor vehicle without displaying "L" plates or when not under the supervision of a qualified driver – both matters being in breach of the conditions of the provisional licence – again, regardless of his reasons for so doing, he commits the two offences. Where the offence is absolute in the sense described, the reasons for committing such offences are relevant only to mitigation which may have an effect on the sentence passed by the court. For example, if before setting out on his journey with a qualified driver a provisional driving licence holder affixes "L" plates conspicuously to the front and to the rear of his vehicle and, unknown to him, one of the "L" plates falls from his vehicle during the course of his journey, he would still commit the offence of "no 'L' plates". If he had the misfortune to be prosecuted for that offence, he would have no defence and his appropriate plea would be one of guilty. However, if in his mitigation before sentence is passed he satisfies the court of the above circumstances, the appropriate sentence for the court to pass would be an absolute discharge – no punishment for what has amounted to a technical offence.

In construction and use offences in respect of motor vehicles, such as defective tyres, defective brakes or defective steering, it is a defence to any of those offences if the defendant proves to the court on the balance of probabilities that he neither knew, nor had reasonable cause to suspect, the existence of the particular defect.

Magistrates should always be alert to the matters alleged against a defendant. Quite often, euphemism is brought into the proceedings which may appear to lessen the seriousness of matters before the court. Stealing from shops is often referred to as "shop-lifting": shop-lifting is stealing, stealing is theft and theft is a crime. Robbery is often referred to as "mugging". The seriousness of robbery may be seen from the definition given above. The court should not be in any doubt as to the seriousness.

Commencement of courtroom procedure

Summary offence

Where the defendant attends court in respect of a summary offence, the procedure, with some slight variations as between courts, is usually as follows:

(1) The legal adviser will ask the defendant to give his name, address and date of birth.

(2) Most legal advisers will ask the defendant if he is ready to proceed with the case or wishes to have time to consult a solicitor or seek an adjournment of the proceedings for some other good reason.

(3) If the defendant is asking for an adjournment to seek the advice of a solicitor or for some other good reason, the court will ordinarily grant an adjournment, fixing the date

and time for the case to be relisted and for the defendant to return to court.

(4) If no adjournment is requested by the defendant or by the prosecution, the legal adviser will read the alleged offence(s) to the defendant and ask him whether he pleads guilty or not guilty. If he pleads guilty, the prosecutor will give the court details of the offence(s) – the "facts" – and anything that is known about the defendant such as any previous convictions, domestic situation and employment. The defendant or his advocate, if he has obtained legal representation, may then address the court in mitigation with any relevant details of the defendant's situation.

(5) If the court does not require any further information, it may then proceed to sentence. If any further information is required, the court will adjourn the proceedings for that purpose.

(6) If the defendant pleads not guilty, the court will fix a trial date, having checked with both the defendant or his advocate and the prosecution as to the availability of their witnesses and the amount of time needed for the trial. Thereafter, the proceedings are adjourned to the trial date, the defendant being told to return on that date or being bailed or remanded in custody as the case may be.

(7) On the date of trial, the procedure is as shown in Diagram A. Where the court dismisses the case, the defendant may or may not apply for costs and thereafter is free to leave the court. If he is found guilty, the procedure thereafter is the same as when a defendant pleads guilty.

Either-way offence

The initial procedure is the same as (1)–(3) above for summary offences. Thereafter the procedure is as follows:

(1) The legal adviser will ask the defendant or his advocate whether the prosecution has provided "advance information", that is, detailed information about the evidence in the possession of the prosecution relating to the case before the court. If advance information has not been given, the court may grant an adjournment for that to be done, if the defendant or his advocate so require. The

Diagram A – Procedure on summary trial

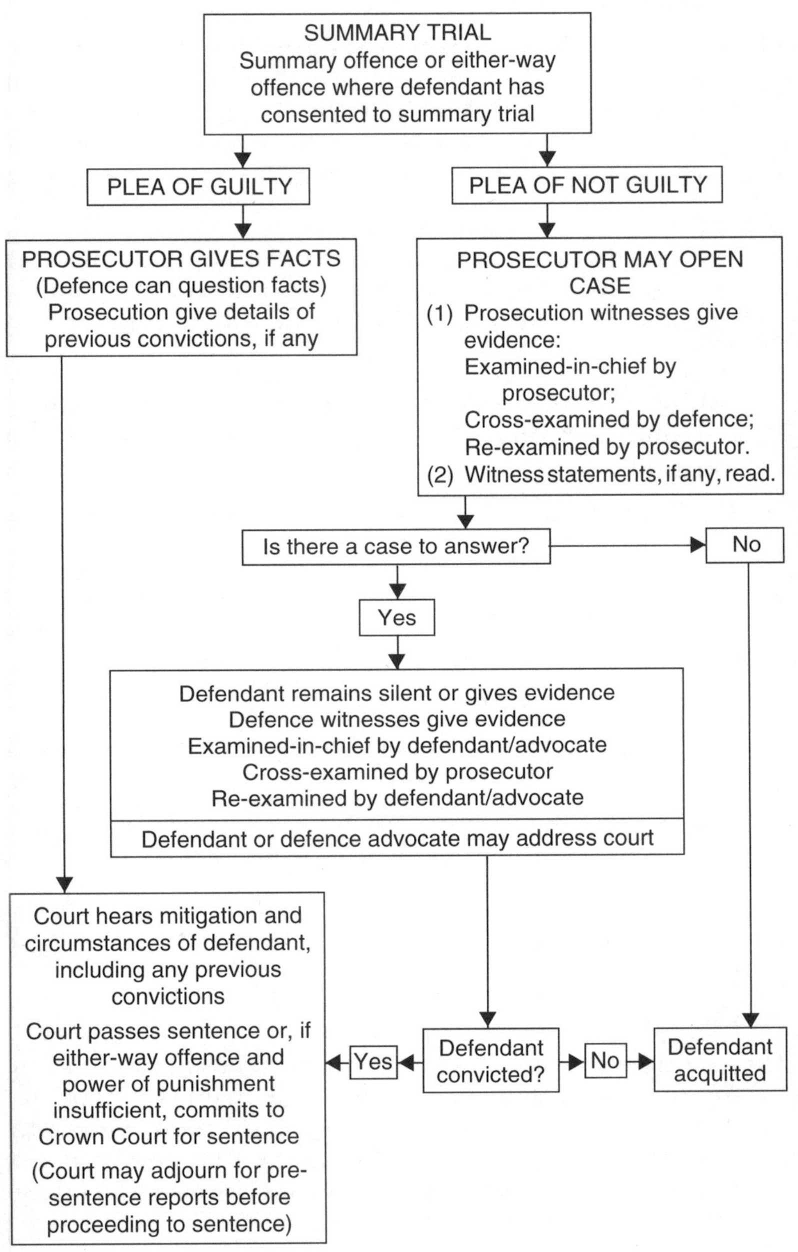

advance information may be in the form of written statements or a précis of the evidence.

(2) Thereafter, the legal adviser will read the alleged offence (the "charge") to the defendant and ask him to indicate if it is his intention to plead guilty or not guilty. If he indicates a plea of guilty, the procedure will be the same as that for a summary offence where the defendant has pleaded guilty.

(3) If the defendant indicates a plea of not guilty or refuses to indicate his plea, the court will conduct what is called the "mode of trial" procedure to determine in which court – the Magistrates' Court or the Crown Court – the case is to be tried. That procedure is as follows:

(a) the prosecutor makes representations as to which court should try the case based on the facts of the alleged offence and its seriousness as seen by the prosecution;

(b) the defendant or his advocate is given a similar opportunity;

(c) the court then decides which court would be more suitable to try the case. The factors which the magistrates must take into account in that process are:

(i) the nature of the case;

(ii) whether the circumstances make the offence a serious one;

(iii) whether the punishment a Magistrates' Court has power to impose would be adequate;

(iv) any other circumstances which make it more suitable for the offence to be tried in one way or the other.

(See Diagram B.)

(4) In coming to a decision, the magistrates will be assisted by Mode of Trial guidelines which have been issued by the Lord Chief Justice which, in respect of many either-way offences, indicate the circumstances of those offences which will favour trial in the Crown Court or trial by the magistrates. (See page 50 below.)

Diagram B – Mode of trial: procedure (MCA 1980, ss. 19-21)

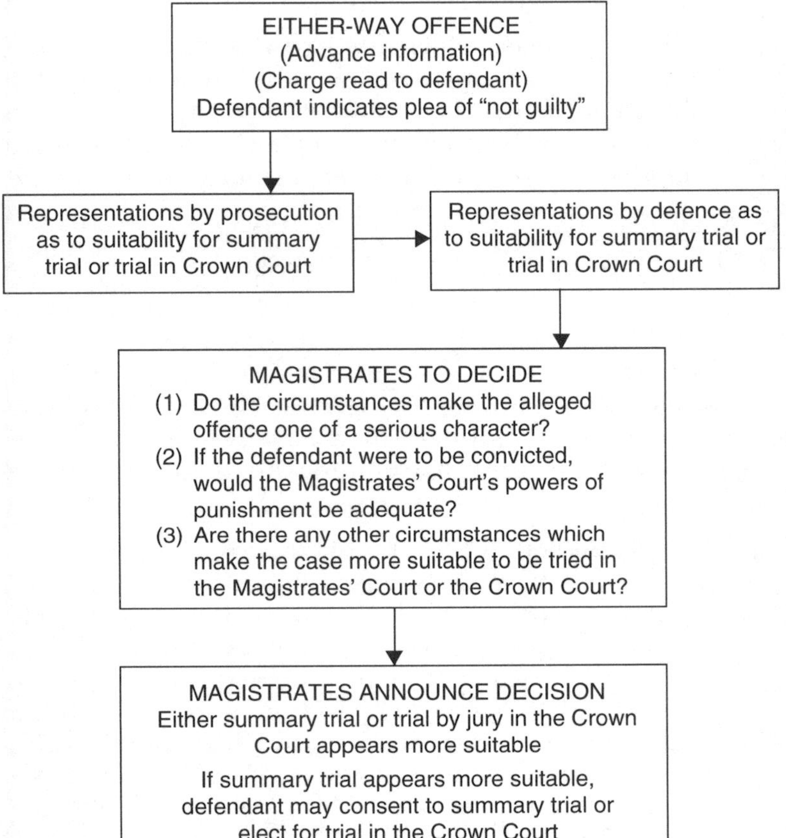

(Note: Mode of trial proceedings are concerned with the *nature of the offence* and *not* the *character* of the defendant. Therefore, any previous convictions of the defendant must neither be disclosed nor considered.)

(5) If the magistrates decide that the case is more suitable for trial in the Crown Court, they will announce that fact and the proceedings will be adjourned (usually for between four and six weeks) for the committal documents to be prepared. If the magistrates decide that the case is more suitable for trial in the Magistrates' Court, they again will

announce that fact. Thereafter the procedure is as follows:

(a) the legal adviser explains to the defendant that it appears to the court that it is more suitable for him to be tried in the Magistrates' Court and that he can consent to be so tried or, if he wishes, he may elect to be tried by a jury in the Crown Court; further, that if he wishes to be tried in the Magistrates' Court and consents to that course and changes his intended plea to guilty or is found guilty after trial in the Magistrates' Court, the magistrates then sitting will be told all that is known about him – his character, any previous convictions ("antecedents") and any other relevant matters – and, if on hearing those matters the magistrates consider their powers of punishment insufficient, they may commit the defendant to the Crown Court for sentence;

(b) the defendant will then be asked to say where he wishes to be tried. If he wishes to be tried in the Crown Court, the proceedings will be adjourned to a later date (usually for between four and six weeks) for the relevant committal documents to be prepared. He will then be remanded on bail or in custody, as appropriate. If he consents to summary trial in the Magistrates' Court, his plea will then be confirmed. If he then indicates a plea of guilty or maintains his plea of not guilty, the procedure is the same as that for a summary offence (see Diagram A, page 37).

Indictable offence

If a prosecution for an indictable offence is to continue, the magistrates can neither accept a plea to the alleged offence nor conduct a trial in respect of it: the matter must go before the Crown Court to be dealt with. The proceedings terminate in the Magistrates' Court by the magistrates "sending" the defendant for trial in the Crown Court on the defendant's first appearance in the Magistrates' Court or after a second or subsequent appearance if for good reason the proceedings have to be adjourned. The court simply announces that the defendant is being committed to the Crown Court to be dealt with and then decides whether the defendant will be sent in custody or on bail. The procedure for deciding whether the defendant is to be sent in custody or on bail is the same as when the court is adjourning summary proceedings.

Procedure in the Magistrates' Court after a plea of not guilty: summary and either-way offences (Diagram A, page 37)

The steps in the trial of a defendant who has pleaded not guilty are as follows:

(1) The prosecutor *may* make an opening speech, outlining what the case is about.

(2) The prosecutor calls his witnesses, each of whom:

(a) is examined-in-chief by the prosecutor;

(b) may be cross-examined by the defendant or his advocate;

(c) may be re-examined by the prosecutor.

The prosecutor may also read the statement of a witness instead of calling the witness to give evidence. The defendant or his advocate must, however, be agreeable to that.

(3) The prosecutor announces that the case for the prosecution is closed.

(4) The defendant or his advocate may then submit that the defendant has "no case to answer".

(5) The prosecutor may reply to any point of law (but not to anything about the facts) raised by the defendant or his advocate at the end of the submission.

(6) The defendant or his advocate may then reply.

(7) The magistrates rule on the submission.

(8) If no submission is made or the magistrates rule that there is a case to answer, the defendant or his advocate may make an opening speech.

(9) The defendant may then give evidence and thereafter call his witnesses, if any, who go through the same procedure as for prosecution witnesses.

(10) The prosecutor may, in limited circumstances, call evidence to rebut what has been said by the defendant in evidence.

(11) The defendant or his advocate may then close the defence case and make a closing speech.

(12) The magistrates decide on their verdict.

(13) The chairman announces the verdict.

(14) If the defendant is acquitted, he may apply for his costs and is released.

(15) If the defendant is convicted, the magistrates are told of any previous convictions of the defendant and may, if reports are required, remand him on bail or in custody for their preparation.

(16) If reports are not required, the defendant or his advocate may address the magistrates about sentence.

(17) After the magistrates have considered and agreed on the sentence, the chairman announces it.

The prosecutor's opening speech

Unless the law involved or the facts that support the charge are complicated, a prosecutor does not always make an opening speech. If, however, he makes reference to the law involved, he must tell the magistrates all the law that is pertinent to the case, including any law which is adverse to his own case and helpful to the defendant. When the law is complicated, the prosecutor should deal with each matter that he must prove against the defendant. If the prosecutor wishes to relate facts, he should state merely a précis of the evidence he will call.

The purpose of a prosecutor's speech is to inform and not persuade the magistrates. What a prosecutor states in his opening speech is not evidence and must never be treated as such by magistrates. At best he states what he hopes to prove.

Calling the prosecutor's witnesses

Witnesses give their evidence having taken the oath or affirmed from the witness box. Sometimes, witnesses are not required to testify in court but instead have their statements read to the court.

Witnesses give evidence or their statements are read in sequence.

Examination-in-chief

Each prosecution witness is first questioned by the prosecutor, the purpose of which is to induce the witness to give his story.

Cross-examination

After examination-in-chief, the defendant or his advocate may ask the witness questions about those parts of his testimony with which the defendant disagrees, since it is a general rule of law that, when a defendant or his advocate does not cross-examine a witness, he accepts as truthful the testimony of that witness.

In effect, cross-examination is necessary:

(a) when the witness has said something the defendant will disagree with or deny; or

(b) when the witness is thought to have information in addition to that which he has related.

The fact that a witness is not cross-examined does not indicate weakness: it is merely that the testimony of the witness is accepted as true.

The defendant or his advocate must test the recollection and truthfulness of the prosecution witnesses, but he must not put to them a different version of events unless the defendant will later substantiate that different version in giving evidence.

Re-examination

After cross-examination, the prosecutor may re-examine the witness.

When re-examining his witness, the prosecutor must confine his questions to matters that were the subject of cross-examination.

Questions by the court

Magistrates must be careful not to assume the mantle of the prosecution or defence advocates by asking questions that go further than clarifying what a witness has said in evidence. For good order, any question by the magistrates should be asked through the chairman and at the end of the witness's evidence. If, as the result of a question asked by the magistrates, the advocates need to ask further questions of the witness, the court should allow them to do so.

Identification of the defendant

It is often the situation in a criminal case that the defendant does not dispute that a crime has occurred but disputes that he is the person who committed the crime. In that situation, it is for the prosecution to establish by admissible evidence that the defendant is the offender. Identity may be established in a number of ways: sometimes identity parades have been held and evidence may be adduced of them and their result. What is not permissible is for a witness to be asked if the person in the dock in the courtroom is the person who committed the offence. Since the defendant is in the dock and in a prominent position, the witness might point to him in any event. That would be manifestly unfair to the defendant.

Submission of "no case to answer"

When all the prosecution witnesses have given evidence and any witness statements read, the prosecutor will indicate that he has reached the end of his case. At this stage, the defendant or, if represented, his advocate may submit that the prosecutor has failed to make out a case against the defendant and that the defendant, therefore, has no case to answer.

The submission may be made where the defendant or his advocate consider that:

(a) there has been no evidence adduced by the prosecution that establishes one or more of the essential elements of the alleged offence; or

(b) the evidence adduced by the prosecution has been so discredited as a result of cross-examination or is so manifestly unreliable that no reasonable tribunal, properly directed on law, could convict on it.

In effect, it is a submission that, according to the law (statutes or regulations or decided cases) or on the evidence called by the prosecution or on both, the prosecution has failed to make out a case against the defendant or that the evidence is unreliable.

The prosecutor may reply to the submission, but in terms of the law only and must confine any reply to legal arguments.

If the defendant's advocate does not make a submission or the defendant is not represented, the magistrates should mentally check that there is evidence that could establish all the elements of the alleged offence. This is particularly important in respect of the unrepresented defendant as he is unlikely to understand that part of the trial procedure.

If the submission is successful, or if the magistrates themselves decide that there is no case to answer, the magistrates must dismiss the case and the defendant will be acquitted. If the submission is unsuccessful, the trial will continue and proceed to the defence case.

A most important matter to note is that, in finding a case to answer, the magistrates are not finding the defendant guilty of the offence: it is simply a stage at which the magistrates are in effect saying that there is evidence which allows the case to proceed. There have been occasions at that stage of the proceedings when the chairman of the court has said that the magistrates have found the case proved, that is, they have found the defendant guilty. Should this occur the trial would have to be stopped and a new trial ordered before different magistrates.

As a guide, at the end of the prosecution case, the chairman should clarify with the defendant or his advocate the stage the proceedings have reached, that is to say, whether:

(a) an opening address is being made; or

(b) a submission of "no case to answer" is being made; or

(c) a final submission or address is being made with the intention of not calling the defendant or witnesses to give evidence.

Even if the magistrates decide that the defendant has a case to answer, they are still a very long way from finding that he is guilty. The defendant is still innocent and it continues to be the prosecution's responsibility to prove that he is guilty beyond reasonable doubt.

If a submission of no case to answer is successful, the magistrates will announce that the defendant is not guilty and, if he is not being held for any other reasons, he is free to leave the court.

If the submission is not successful, the trial continues and then moves to the defence case.

The defence case: the defendant's right to give evidence

After the conclusion of the prosecution case or after an unsuccessful submission of no case to answer, the defendant has the following choices: he may call no evidence at all, in which case he may make a final submission; or he may without giving evidence himself, call witnesses; or may give evidence himself with or without calling witnesses.

Where the defendant is not represented by an advocate, the court must inform the defendant that he has the right to remain silent or give evidence and call witnesses. He must be warned that, if he chooses not to give evidence or if he decides to give evidence and when doing so refuses for no good reason to answer any question put to him, the court may draw such inferences it considers appropriate from the failure to give evidence or to answer a question. If the defendant is represented, those matters need not be mentioned by the court if the defence advocate says that the defendant will give evidence. Otherwise the court must ensure that the advocate has advised the defendant of the matters the court would have mentioned to the defendant had he not been represented. If the defence advocate has not advised the defendant in respect of these matters, the court will direct him to do so and may adjourn the proceedings for a while for that to be done.

If the defendant gives evidence, he and any witnesses he calls will give their evidence in similar form to the prosecution witnesses: examination-in-chief, cross-examination by the prosecution and re-examination.

The closing of the defendant's case

After all the defence evidence has been given, the defendant or his advocate will close the case and may then make a final speech.

During his final speech, the defendant or his advocate may argue that in law the defendant is not guilty. He may emphasise those parts of the law that favour his contention, but he must not misquote the law nor mislead the magistrates as to what is the law.

He may stress the parts of, and omissions from, the evidence that favour the defendant and draw the magistrates' attention to any inconsistencies in that evidence. He must not, of course, distort or mislead the magistrates as to what was said.

The advocate must remember also that he is an advocate and not a witness. He must base his arguments on only the evidence given during the trial; he may not introduce new information.

The magistrates' decision

At the conclusion of the defence speech, the magistrates will proceed to consider their verdict. They may only convict the defendant if the prosecution has proved the defendant's guilt beyond reasonable doubt. If this is not the situation, they must acquit the defendant. If they believe the defence evidence on a balance of probabilities, that is to say that the evidence is more likely to be true than not, they should acquit the defendant. The magistrates should approach these decisions with the same common sense that they use in everyday problems. Where there are sensible doubts, the defendant must be acquitted.

Magistrates can only act on the evidence that has been put before them and they must not speculate or consider any matter extraneous to the case. It is important for them to remember that a police officer's evidence is to be treated in the same manner as any other witness's evidence and that the officer's evidence has no special value because the officer happens to be in uniform or is called by the prosecution. Neither do the defendant and his witnesses have a lower value merely because he is the person accused of a crime and the witnesses are called by him.

When magistrates retire to consider their verdict, each one must make his own decision but the final decision must be that of the magistrates collectively: although there may be a majority verdict of two to one, the verdict must be presented as that of all three magistrates. The chairman has no second or casting vote and should ensure that the deliberations are controlled and that nothing extraneous enters the discussion. Obviously, the magistrates will listen with care to their colleagues' views and express their own views but they must make their individual decisions. If two magistrates only are trying a case and they are unable to agree on a verdict one way or the other, the case will have to be retried by a different Bench.

Where there is more than one charge against the defendant or there are two or more defendants being tried together, a separate verdict must be reached in respect of each charge and each defendant. The fact that magistrates may acquit a defendant on one charge does not necessarily mean that he is innocent of the remaining charge(s), nor does the conviction of one defendant mean that the others are guilty.

A magistrate can only act judicially if he is confident that any disputes that take place in the retiring room will not later be the subject of amused or critical comment. No matter how vehemently magistrates may argue and disagree over a decision, what is said in the retiring room should be forgotten and remain secret once the decision is given.

Announcing the decision

On return to court after making their decision, the chairman should announce the decision in respect of each charge and each defendant, announcing the verdict in the form of "guilty" or "not guilty".

Request of costs by acquitted defendant

A defendant who is found not guilty may ask that he be awarded the costs of his defence. Such costs would include pre-court work in preparation for the trial and for the trial itself, together with any interim hearings. The fact that a defendant is acquitted is not, in itself, a reason why he should be awarded his costs: the magistrates have a discretion which must be exercised judicially as to whether or not the defendant should be awarded costs. If, for example, a defendant brought the case upon himself and had misled the police to believe that the case against him was stronger than it was, the magistrates would be entitled to refuse the defendant an award of costs.

If the magistrates agree to award costs, they make what is known as a "defendant's costs order" and the costs are paid out of Central Funds, that is the amount of money set aside by Parliament for payment of such matters. If the amount of costs cannot be agreed, the defence advocate will be required to submit his bill to the justices' clerk for "taxation": for the clerk or some other authorised court official to decide how much of the costs should be paid. On a personal basis, the defendant can only claim for travelling expenses and subsistence and not loss of earnings. Defence costs may also be awarded when no evidence is offered in the case by the prosecution, the proceedings are withdrawn or discontinued or the defendant is discharged in committal proceedings.

If a defendant has had the benefit of a legal representation order (formerly known as a legal aid order), he will not be able to claim costs from Central Funds, save the costs of travel and subsistence.

Procedure – defendant found guilty

If the defendant is found guilty, the magistrates must consider whether to deal with sentence there and then or to adjourn for a pre-sentence report or other information they consider to be relevant before the appropriate sentence is decided upon (see Diagram B, page 39). If adjourning for reports, the magistrates must remand the defendant upon bail or in custody until date of sentence which may only be for a maximum of 21 days if the defendant is to be in custody or 28 days if he is on bail.

Thus, in summary, within a trial it is the magistrates' function to listen to the evidence and decide on the facts which are in dispute between the parties and, together with any facts that are agreed by the parties, to apply the law to those facts and reach a verdict. In the event of a conviction in a trial or a plea of guilty, the magistrates are required to pass sentence, impose an order or deal with the matter in some other way authorised by law. That may happen at the time of conviction or on a subsequent occasion if the magistrates consider that they need further information about the defendant before they are able, properly, to decide what the appropriate sentence or order should be.

National Mode of Trial Guidelines 1995

When considering where an either-way offence should be tried (see Diagram B, page 39), it is important for magistrates to inform themselves as much as possible of the seriousness of the alleged offence. Decisions as to the mode of trial should not be made on the grounds of expedience or convenience. Only the seriousness of the alleged offence is relevant and, for the purpose of deciding mode of trial, magistrates should assume that the prosecution version of the facts is correct: the defendant's antecedents and personal mitigation are irrelevant and the magistrates are not entitled to know of the defendant's criminal convictions.

Where cases involve complex questions of fact or difficult questions of law, magistrates should always consider committing the case for trial in the Crown Court.

Generally, either-way offences should be tried summarily unless the magistrates consider that:

(a) the particular case has one or more of the features set out below; *and*

(b) their powers of sentence would be insufficient.

Note: In the following lists, "high value" means at least twice the amount of the limit imposed by statute on a Magistrates' Court when making a compensation order – currently £5,000.

Burglary – dwelling house

(1) Entry in the daytime when the occupier (or another) is present.

(2) Entry at night of a house which is normally occupied, whether or not the occupier or another is present.

(3) The offence is alleged to be one of a series of similar offences.

(4) When soiling, ransacking, damage or vandalism occurs.

(5) The offence has professional hallmarks.

(6) The unrecovered property is of high value.

Offences of burglary in a dwelling house *cannot* be tried summarily if any person in the dwelling house was subjected to violence or to threats of violence (MCA 1980, Schedule 1, paragraph 28(c)).

Burglary – non-dwellings

(1) Entry of a pharmacy or doctor's surgery.

(2) Fear is caused or violence is done to any person lawfully on the premises (e.g. night watchman or security guard).

(3) The offence has professional hallmarks.

(4) Vandalism on a substantial scale.

(5) The unrecovered property is of high value.

Theft and fraud

(1) Breach of trust by a person in a position of substantial authority, or in whom a high degree of trust is placed.

(2) Theft or fraud which has been committed by an organised gang.

(3) The victim is particularly vulnerable to theft or fraud, e.g. elderly or infirm.

(4) The unrecovered property is of high value.

Handling stolen goods

(1) By a receiver who has commissioned the theft.

(2) The offence has professional hallmarks.

(3) The unrecovered property is of high value.

Social Security frauds

(1) Organised fraud on a large scale.

(2) The frauds are substantial and carried out over a long period of time.

Violence: wounding and actual bodily harm

(1) The use of a weapon likely to cause serious injury.

(2) A weapon is used and serious injury is caused.

(3) More than minor injury is caused by kicking, head butting or similar forms of assault.

(4) Serious violence is caused to those whose work has to be done in contact with the public, e.g. police officers, bus drivers, taxi drivers, publicans and shopkeepers.

(5) Violence to vulnerable persons, e.g. the elderly and infirm.

The same considerations apply to domestic violence.

Public order offences – violent disorder

These should generally be committed to the Crown Court for trial.

Public order offences – affray

(1) Organised violence or use of weapons.

(2) Significant injury or substantial damage.

(3) The offence has clear racial motivation.

(4) An attack on police officers, ambulance personnel, firefighters and the like.

Violence to, and neglect of, children

(1) Substantial injury.

(2) Repeated violence or serious neglect, even if the harm is slight.

(3) Sadistic violence, e.g. deliberate burning or scalding.

Indecent assault

(1) Substantial disparity in age between victim and accused, and the assault is more than trivial.

(2) Violence or threats of violence.

(3) Relationship of trust or responsibility between accused and victim.

(4) Several similar offences and the assaults are more than trivial.

(5) The victim is particularly vulnerable.

(6) Serious nature of the assault.

Unlawful sexual intercourse

(1) Wide disparity of age.

(2) Breach of position of trust.

(3) The victim is particularly vulnerable.

Unlawful sexual intercourse with a girl under 13 is triable on indictment only.

Drugs – Class A

(1) Supply, possession with intent to supply should be transferred for trial.

(2) Possession cases should be transferred for trial unless amount is small and consistent only with personal use.

Drugs – Class B

(1) Supply, possession with intent to supply should be transferred for trial unless there is only small scale supply for no payment.

(2) Possession cases should be transferred for trial when the quantity is substantial.

Dangerous driving

(1) Alcohol or drugs contributing to recklessness.

(2) Grossly excessive speed.

(3) Racing.

(4) Prolonged course of reckless driving.

(5) Other related offences.

Criminal damage

(1) Deliberate fire-raising.

(2) Committed by a group.

(3) Damage of a high value.

(4) Offence has clear racial motivation.

Chapter 9

LEGAL REPRESENTATION

A party to any proceedings in a Magistrates' Court may be represented by a legal representative, that is to say, by a barrister or by a solicitor. Prosecutions on behalf of the Crown are undertaken by members of the Crown Prosecution Service or their agents or designated case workers. Employees of certain organisations may be authorised to undertake prosecutions on behalf of their organisation, for example the Health and Safety Executive, British Transport authorities and Departments of State such as the Benefits Agency and HM Customs and Excise.

In a private prosecution, such as a neighbour dispute which leads to a charge of assault, the prosecutor can conduct the court proceedings himself; he is not obliged to be legally represented. Likewise, a defendant need not be legally represented but may employ a solicitor to act for him.

The magistrates do have a limited discretion to allow someone else to act on behalf of either party but right of audience is normally restricted to the parties or their legal representatives. If a child or young person before the Magistrates' Court or the Youth Court is not legally represented, the court must allow his parent, guardian, relative or other responsible person to assist him.

Any person may attend a trial as a "friend" of an unrepresented party and may take notes and generally assist the party, and the magistrates should allow the friend to assist the unrepresented party unless they are satisfied that fairness and the interests of justice do not require that party to have such assistance. The friend has no right to address the court. The court is solely concerned with the interests of the party and, if the magistrates refuse to allow a friend to assist the party, they should give their reasons for that decision. When allowed, the friend in these situations is often referred to as a "McKenzie friend".

The Legal Services Commission is responsible for the provision of publicly funded legal services and the establishment of the Criminal Defence Service. The purpose of the service is to secure that individuals who are involved in criminal investigations or criminal proceedings have access to legal advice, assistance and representation. Statute has established a framework for those matters and the statutory provisions must be given effect in a manner compatible with the Human Rights Act 1998 and Convention rights. Article 6(3)(c) of the Convention provides that everyone who is charged with a criminal offence has the right to defend himself in person or by legal assistance of his own choosing or, if he has not sufficient means to pay for the legal assistance, to be given assistance free of charge when the interests of justice so require.

The Legal Services Commission provides for duty solicitors to attend at Magistrates' Courts for the purpose of providing assistance by way of representation to defendants or of giving advice and assistance to them where the defendants are not otherwise receiving representation. The assistance may be given:

(a) in making a bail application;

(b) at an appearance in court where the defendant is in custody and wishes the case to be concluded at that appearance, unless the solicitor considers that the case should be adjourned in the interests of justice or the defendant;

(c) if the defendant is before the court for failure to obey an order of the court where such failure may lead to the defendant being at risk of imprisonment;

(d) if the defendant is not in custody but in the opinion of the solicitor he requires assistance.

Assistance by way of representation by a duty solicitor is not available in proceedings where the defendant pleads not guilty. It is not available in proceedings in connection with a non-imprisonable offence unless the solicitor considers the circumstances to be exceptional. Assistance may be given to a fine-defaulter or offender who has defaulted in payment of any other sum ordered on conviction, but only where the failure to pay may lead to a risk of imprisonment.

Assistance from a duty solicitor is provided without reference to a defendant's financial circumstances and is given free of cost.

A defendant charged with, or convicted of, an offence may apply to the court for a legal representation order (formerly referred to as legal aid). If the application is granted, the order will extend, as appropriate, to any preliminary proceedings or incidental proceedings such as a bail application. The order also includes advice and assistance for the purpose of an appeal. The court may only grant the application where it appears desirable to do so in the interests of justice and in some specified cases where the defendant's financial resources are such that he is eligible for representation. The factors to be taken into account in determining whether it is the "interests of justice" to grant a legal representation order include:

(a) the offence is such that, if proved, it is likely that the court would impose a sentence which would deprive the defendant of his liberty or lead to a loss of livelihood or serious damage to his reputation;

(b) the determination of the case may involve consideration of a substantial question of law;

(c) the defendant may be unable to understand the proceedings or to state his own case because of his inadequate knowledge of English, mental illness or other mental or physical disability;

(d) the nature of the defence is such as to involve the tracing and interviewing of witnesses or expert cross-examination of a witness for the prosecution;

(e) it is in the interests of someone other than the defendant that the defendant be represented.

The application for a legal representation order has to be made to the justices' clerk in a prescribed form or orally to the court. The justices' clerk has power to grant or refuse the application on the first occasion that it is made. A refusal may only be made on the grounds that it does not appear desirable in the interests of justice to grant it and/or, in the few cases where means have to be considered, that the defendant's disposable income and disposable capital are such that the defendant is ineligible for a legal representation order. An application may be renewed orally to the court or the justices' clerk. A renewed application may be granted by the justices' clerk or he may refer it to a magistrate to consider.

The legal representation order provides for representation by a solicitor. In the case of an indictable offence where the court is of the opinion that the circumstances of the case make it unusually grave or difficult, the order may include representation by both solicitor and counsel (a barrister). Ordinarily, a defendant who is granted a representation order may choose - and shall be assigned - any solicitor who is willing to act for him.

Since 2nd October 2000, it has not been necessary for Magistrates' Courts to carry out a means test for legal representation in many cases which have been charged by the police and in all cases that are to go before a Youth Court. The legislation now provides that, where a person is charged at a police station with an offence, other than an indictable only offence or an offence that will be sent to the Crown Court under section 51 of the Crime and Disorder Act 1998, any application to a Magistrates' Court for the grant of legal representation will not be means tested. Where these criteria apply or where the case is to go before a Youth Court, the only test that will be applied is the interests of justice test. The means test will apply to cases which, in the case of an adult, are begun by way of a summons.

Chapter 10

THE ADVOCATES

For proceedings in the courtroom to be efficient and orderly, the rules of evidence, procedure and etiquette must be obeyed by everyone taking part in them – including members of the public in the gallery. The chairman must ensure, with the assistance of the legal adviser if necessary, that rules are obeyed and, in doing so, he must know something of the duties and responsibilities of the professional advocates.

The advocate's duty

No matter what type of case the court is dealing with, nor whether acting for the prosecution or the defence, the advocate must, in addition to his responsibilities to his client:

(a) tell the court of all the law that is pertinent to the issue before the court, even that which is unfavourable to his client;

(b) not mislead the court by mentioning matters in an opening speech which witnesses cannot attest to or prove; and

(c) base his arguments on the evidence before the court and not volunteer information that has not been put in evidence.

An advocate may, however, argue that the pertinent law should be interpreted in a manner favourable to his client. Equally, provided he does not distort or wrongly state the testimony of witnesses, he may argue that the testimony must be inaccurate, should not be accepted or should be viewed so as to favour his client.

The obligations of a prosecutor

The prosecutor is to present the prosecution's case against the defendant fairly and it is his duty in that task to assist the court in identifying the issues in the case. The primary duty of the prosecutor is to the court; so long as he has presented the case against the defendant fairly and has tested the defendant's and the defence witnesses' testimony by cross-examination, that duty is discharged – it is not his task to "win at all costs". Should it become obvious or seem probable during the course of a trial that the case against the defendant cannot be sustained, he must not attempt to fabricate a better case but should formally offer no evidence and the case will be dismissed.

Whilst cross-examination of the defendant and his witnesses needs to be searching and analytical, the prosecutor must not mislead nor bully. If he is aware of prosecution witnesses but does not intend to call them to give evidence in a trial, he is obliged to inform the defendant or the solicitors acting for the defendant of that fact and to give the names and addresses of those witnesses. That information should be given to the defence at the earliest opportunity so that, if the defence wish to call those witnesses to give evidence, there is sufficient time for the defence to interview them. The defence, however, are not under a similar obligation to assist the prosecution.

Laymen as prosecutors

A wide variety of people, including Trading Standards Officers, Health and Safety Inspectors and local government officials are permitted by statute to act as prosecutors in Magistrates' Courts' proceedings. But the majority of criminal prosecutions – those which are brought by the State – are conducted and prosecuted by the Crown Prosecution Service. These prosecutors are barristers or solicitors who are full-time paid employees of the Service. Quite often, as a result of insufficient staff levels, Crown prosecutors are unable to conduct trials in the Magistrates' Court and barristers are briefed on an "agency" basis to conduct the prosecutions.

Lay prosecutors have not necessarily had the training and experience of their barrister/solicitor counterparts and may find advocacy a chore or find it difficult to acquire the required objectivity, particularly when a defendant, who they know to be guilty, escapes conviction because of some rule of evidence or a technicality. Although a court may sympathise, it must not favour those prosecutors: those who initiate prosecutions must take the consequences and not rely on the court or the legal adviser to "undertake" the prosecution. The rules of evidence and procedure must be applied strictly whoever the prosecutor might be.

The obligations of a defence advocate

Subject to the general duty of an advocate to inform the court of all the pertinent law, the duty of the defence advocate is to his client. It is his task to put the defendant's version of events giving rise to the criminal charges to the court. Whilst the advocate may advise the defendant that an apparently impossible story is unlikely to be believed, the decision as to any defence the defendant has is, and always must be, that of the defendant. There is one circumstance in which the advocate must not tell or advance his client's story: that is when the defendant admits that his story is false. If the defendant insists on telling that false story, the advocate must refuse to act for him.

The burden of proving a defendant's guilt is on the prosecution and it is to the high standard of proof "beyond reasonable doubt". Thus it is the defence advocate's duty to test the memory and truthfulness of the prosecution witnesses by cross-examination and to ensure that the rules of evidence and procedure are obeyed. He may take advantage of every technicality available to him, as well as inadequacies on the part of the prosecution, and the magistrates should not hold that against him. It is also his duty, quickly and fearlessly but courteously, to protect his client from improper questions or departures from the rules of evidence.

Chapter 11

THE UNREPRESENTED DEFENDANT

The criminal justice procedures are complex and, in some instances, cumbersome. Those procedures are refined and developed by an increasing number of statutes and regulations and are sometimes abolished after a very short time. The procedures must be considered alongside the Human Rights Act 1998 and the Convention on Human Rights and Fundamental Freedoms. These matters are difficult enough for an advocate and may be impossibly so for an unrepresented defendant. Now that legal representation is much more freely available, the number of defendants who are unrepresented in indictable and either-way cases is very few. However, in respect of summary offences, especially road traffic offences, television licence evasion and vehicle excise licence evasion, the vast majority of defendants are unrepresented and it is the magistrates' responsibility to ensure that the defendant fully understands the procedure of the court and has a fair trial.

An advocate not only prepares and presents his client's case but acts as a guide and friend in giving his client confidence and an understanding of what is likely to happen in the courtroom. The unrepresented defendant may be bewildered by the hustle and bustle of the courtroom and, on occasions, by what may appear to be indifference on the part of some people in the courtroom. When these matters are added to his apprehension that the court's decisions could well affect his future life, it is not surprising that he may be on edge and in need of tactful and patient treatment if he is eventually to leave the courtroom believing that he has been fairly treated.

People who have been arrested or summoned to appear before the court are often unfamiliar with court procedure and may arrive at court unprepared for what is to happen. It is essential for the court to ensure that the defendant understands what transpires and to check, for example, whether an adjournment is needed for the defendant to consult a solicitor or apply for a legal representation order; or needs time or an adjournment to consider advance information served on him by the prosecutor. It is also essential for the court to ensure that a defendant understands the charge or allegation made against him. When a trial is to take place, the procedure should be explained at each stage and the defendant informed of his rights within the trial.

Even when the defendant is unrepresented, if he chooses to give evidence, the prosecutor must cross-examine him in the same manner as if he had been represented. The magistrates must, however, ensure that no unfair advantage is taken by the prosecutor. Likewise, no matter how sympathetic the magistrates may be for the defendant's immediate predicament, they must remain impartial. Occasionally, the defendant's inexperience may result in an indignant or angry outburst. Magistrates must be prepared where appropriate to make allowance for that. None of this, however, changes the fact that a defendant cannot be guilty of the offence with which he has been accused unless the magistrates are satisfied of his guilt beyond reasonable doubt.

In a trial situation, it is often difficult for defendants to phrase questions without lapsing into narration. It does not help for the chairman of the magistrates curtly to tell the defendant that he should confine himself to questions when cross-examining prosecution witnesses. Where there is a danger of this happening, there is a positive role for the legal adviser to play in having the defendant narrate his version of events and then transposing narrative into a series of questions. Inevitably, the trial of an unrepresented defendant takes more time and the role of the magistrates and their legal adviser is more difficult. It is for that reason that the true worth of the magistrates and their adviser is never more discernible than when they are responding to the needs of a defendant.

Chapter 12

EVIDENCE GENERALLY

It is a fundamental principle of the English legal system that a person who is accused of an offence must be judged only on information that is acceptable as evidence and that the evidence is adduced in court in accordance with accepted and established rules. Magistrates are not expected to know the rules by heart – that is why they have legal advisers to assist them and advocates whose duty it is to draw matters to their attention – but they are expected to consider any objection that is raised in respect of any "evidence" that is or is about to be given and to any objection as to the manner in which it is sought to adduce that "evidence". It is within the magistrates' power to exclude evidence which they consider to be inadmissible for good reason.

It has long been a tenet of the legal system that it is preferable that a guilty person is acquitted rather than an innocent person be convicted. It is from this that most of the rules of evidence and procedures in a trial stem.

The burden of proof and the standard of proof

Magistrates and judges are not given an inquisitorial role, that is to say that they do not have a right or duty to conduct an inquiry to unearth the truth during a trial. A trial is conducted under an adversarial system whereby a prosecutor accuses a named individual of being guilty of a specified legal wrong and during the trial the prosecutor attempts to prove, by evidence, his accusation against the defendant. The parties, their advocates and the magistrates are interested only in the particular accusation against the defendant. The general burden or duty of proving that the defendant has committed the offence with which he has been charged is on the prosecutor and there is no burden on the defendant to prove his innocence.

Normally, the burden of proof remains on the prosecutor throughout the trial. It does not vary from crime to crime and the standard of proof required is that the prosecution shall prove a defendant's guilt beyond all reasonable doubt, that is to say, to prove the defendant's guilt to a standard whereby the magistrates are able to say that they are sure of the defendant's guilt. If, at the end of a trial, the magistrates are able to say that they feel sure of the defendant's guilt, they will convict him of the offence for which he is being tried. If they are not able to say that they are satisfied beyond reasonable doubt, it is their duty to dismiss the charge and declare the defendant not guilty.

There are some offences and some occasions where the burden of proof is transferred from the prosecution to the defendant, such as in a trial where the defendant is accused of possessing an offensive weapon or of driving without appropriate insurance cover. When the burden is transferred, it is for the defendant then to prove his innocence. However, the standard of proof in that situation is nothing like as high as that demanded of the prosecutor. All the defendant is required to do is satisfy the magistrates of his innocence on the "balance of probabilities" – that is to say is it more likely than not that what the defendant says is true.

Relevance of evidence

Evidence is the information that tends to help prove or disprove the issue before the court – whether the defendant has committed the offence or not – and any other information that does not satisfy that requirement must be excluded. For example, if a defendant is charged with theft and the prosecution says that there has been a wave of theft in the area, that is of no relevance and does not go to prove that the defendant is dishonest and has stolen. Again, if on arrest for that offence the defendant swore at the police officer, it goes to prove nothing more than that the defendant was discourteous. There is a need for magistrates to be on guard against being influenced by irrelevant and inadmissible information.

If either the prosecution or the defence are unable to put certain factual information before the court in the form of a witness's evidence or a witness's written statement and that information needs to be put in as being of relevance, the prosecutor or the defence may make what is called "a formal admission of fact" which has to be recorded in writing and signed by the person making the admission. That document will then form part of the evidence in the case. For example, the defendant may be charged with taking a motor vehicle without the owner's permission. The prosecutor is expecting the owner to attend court to give evidence that the vehicle belonged to him and that it was taken without his permission but the owner does not arrive at court. The defence do not dispute that the particular vehicle was taken by someone without permission: the only issue in the trial is "did this defendant take the vehicle?" In such circumstances, rather than having the trial adjourned to another day for the owner to give evidence, the defence may well make a formal admission that it is accepted by the defence that the vehicle was taken without its owner's permission (see page 69).

Leading questions

A leading question is one which:

(a) is so phrased as to suggest the answer required; and

(b) is asked about something that is in issue between the parties.

Neither the prosecution nor the defence is allowed to ask leading questions when examining-in-chief or during re-examination of a witness they have called to give evidence. The point is that, if the answer required is given as a result of a leading question, that information is worthless and is not part of the evidence.

Leading questions may be asked in cross-examination and the purpose is either to discredit the witness or cause him to say something which may be of assistance to the other party to the case.

Police officers, notebooks and witness notes

Normally, a witness must give evidence without reference to any written notes or a statement made by him. Police officers, when called to give evidence, are no different to any other witnesses, they are not "professional" witnesses and do not enjoy any privilege or special treatment by the court.

A witness may refer to any notes made by him for the purpose of refreshing his memory of matters to which the notes relate, provided:

(a) the witness has some memory, without reference to the notes, of the incidents; and

(b) the notes were made at the time of, or shortly after, the incidents to which they relate and the events were still fresh in the witness's mind.

If the court allows the witness to refresh his memory from the notes, that is all he is permitted to do: he cannot read his notes aloud to the court and seek to have them treated as his evidence. If a witness has no memory to refresh, he may not substitute his notes for his memory.

Hearsay evidence

Generally, a witness may only give evidence of what he saw with his own eyes or heard with his own ears and may not repeat what he was told by a third party.

Like most legal rules, there are some exceptions to it and the legal adviser will guide the magistrates when an exception to the rule arises. One exception often arises: ordinarily a witness may not tell the court what he said to, or heard from, another person. If, however, the conversation took place in the presence and hearing of the defendant, details of the conversation, if relevant to the proceedings, can be given to the court. The conversation cannot be given as evidence of the truth of what was said. It is given so that the magistrates may judge, from the response of the defendant to what is said, the extent to which the defendant accepts the truth of it.

A defendant's previous convictions

Ordinarily, no reference must be made during a trial to any previous conviction a defendant may have. There are exceptional situations when, with leave of the court, a defendant's convictions may be put in evidence – but these situations do not often arise and must be dealt with most carefully with guidance from the legal adviser. The main examples are where the defendant has said in his evidence that he has no previous convictions when the reverse is in fact true; or where the defence has attacked the character or credibility of a prosecution witness.

On occasions, when the defendant is called to give evidence, his advocate asks him to tell the court if he is of previous good character, that is to say, has no previous convictions. This is a perfectly proper question if in fact the defendant does not have convictions. However, magistrates must be aware that if such a question is not put to the defendant by his advocate it must *not* be assumed that the defendant does have previous convictions. Such a question must not be asked of the defendant by the prosecution, save in exceptional situations as referred to above.

There are far more rules of evidence than are mentioned here. For all those rules as to what may or may not be received in court as evidence, it remains the function of the magistrates as to what or whom they believe or do not believe and to be able to give reasons for the belief or disbelief.

Evidence by written statements

In a criminal trial, the written statement made by any person is admissible in evidence to the same extent as oral evidence by that person, provided the following conditions are satisfied:

(1) The statement purports to be signed by the person who made it.

(2) The statement contains a declaration by that person to the effect that:

  (a) it is true to the best of his knowledge and belief;

  (b) he made the statement knowing that, if it were tendered in evidence, he would be liable to prosecution if he wilfully stated in it anything which he knew to be false or did not believe to be true.

(3) Before the hearing at which the statement is to be tendered in evidence, a copy of the statement is served by, or on behalf of, the party proposing to tender it, as soon as is practicable, on:

  (a) the clerk to the justices;

(b) each of other parties to the proceedings (even on those who are unaffected by the contents of the statement).

(4) None of the other parties or their solicitors, within seven days from the service of the copy of the statement, serves notice on the party proposing to tender the statement, objecting to the statement being tendered in evidence.

The conditions mentioned in paragraphs (3) and (4) need not be observed so long as all the parties agree either before or during the hearing.

Whenever a written statement is tendered instead of the witness giving evidence in person:

(a) if the statement is made by a person under the age of twenty-one, it shall give his age;

(b) if it is made by a person who cannot read, it shall be read to him before he signs it and shall be accompanied by a declaration by the person who read the statement to the effect that it was so read;

(c) if it refers to any other document as an exhibit, the copy served on the clerk to the justices and any other party to the proceedings shall be accompanied by a copy of that document or by such information as may be necessary in order to enable the party on whom it is served to inspect that document or a copy.

Although a written statement may have been correctly prepared and served and no party to the proceedings has objected prior to the hearing to its introduction as evidence, at the hearing the party on whose behalf the statement was served may call the witness to give oral evidence. Furthermore, the magistrates, on the application of any party to the proceedings, may require the maker of the statement to attend court and give oral evidence.

The admissible parts of the statement must be read aloud in court by or on behalf of the party tendering it, unless the court otherwise directs. In this event, an oral account must be given of the parts not read aloud.

The fact that a defendant or other party to the proceedings

does not object to the introduction of a written statement, instead of causing the witness to attend court, means that the defendant or other party is admitting the truth of what the statement contains.

Proof of facts by formal admission

Subject to safeguards, any fact of which oral evidence may be given in any criminal proceedings may be admitted by, or on behalf of, the prosecutor or the defendant. Once such a fact is admitted, it is conclusive evidence in those particular proceedings against the party who made the admission.

An admission may be made before or during the proceedings.

If the admission is not made in court, it must be in writing and, if made by an individual, must be signed by him; while, if it is made by a body corporate, it must be signed by a director, secretary or manager of, or clerk to, the corporate body.

When the admission is made during the proceedings, it must be written down and signed by, or on behalf of, the person making it.

An example would be where, at a trial of a defendant who has pleaded not guilty to taking another person's vehicle without consent, the prosecutor does not have the owner of the vehicle at court to give evidence or a written statement that could be read to establish ownership and that the vehicle has been taken without consent. Rather than having the proceedings adjourned for that evidence to be put before the magistrates, if the defendant does not dispute that the vehicle has been taken without consent but only disputes that he took it, the defendant may make a formal admission of fact in writing accepting that the vehicle had been taken without consent.

A "Newton" hearing

The fact that a defendant pleads guilty to an offence does not necessarily mean that he accepts all the facts as alleged by the prosecution. For example, a motorist may plead guilty to exceeding a speed limit of 30 m.p.h. but the prosecution says that his speed was 50 m.p.h. while the defendant says his speed was 35 m.p.h.; or a defendant admits that he assaulted a victim causing him a broken nose and the prosecution says that he caused that injury by use of a weapon while the defendant says he caused the injury by punching the victim. In such cases, if the difference in the version of the facts would make a material difference to the sentence that the magistrates would impose, the magistrates will have to hear evidence in order to decide which version of the facts it prefers. A court hearing for this matter is commonly referred to as a "Newton" hearing, Newton being the name of the case in which the High Court stated the foregoing procedure should be followed.

Interpreters

If a defendant is unable to understand or communicate in English, the court must provide an interpreter for him, the cost of which is borne by the State. If a witness needs the assistance of an interpreter, it is for the party calling the witness to arrange the attendance of such an interpreter.

Chapter 13

COMMITTAL TO THE CROWN COURT FOR TRIAL OF EITHER-WAY OFFENCES

Before a defendant can stand trial in the Crown Court, he must have been committed there by the magistrates for that purpose. Either-way offences, where the Magistrates' Court has declined to try them or where the defendant has elected trial by jury, become the subject of formal committal proceedings.

There are two forms of committal proceedings:

(1) The "paper" committal - commonly referred to as a Section 6(2) committal (a reference to the section of the Magistrates' Court Act 1980 creating the committal) - where the defendant is committed for trial without the magistrates considering the prosecution evidence.

(2) The "read through" committal - sometimes referred to as a Section 6(1) committal - where the magistrates read the prosecution statements and commit the offender for trial if they consider that there is a case to be tried by a jury. Neither the defendant nor witnesses are called to give evidence in the Magistrates' Court.

The "paper" or Section 6(2) committal

The court is neither required nor permitted to inquire into the prosecution evidence and is simply required to ensure that the following conditions are satisfied:

(a) the defendant must be represented by a barrister or solicitor, although one does not have to be present during the committal proceedings;

(b) all the prosecution evidence must be in the form of written statements and comply with statutory requirements;

(c) the defence must agree that the statements disclose a case against the defendant; and

Diagram C – Committal for trial: MCA 1980, s. 6(2) (committal without consideration of the evidence)

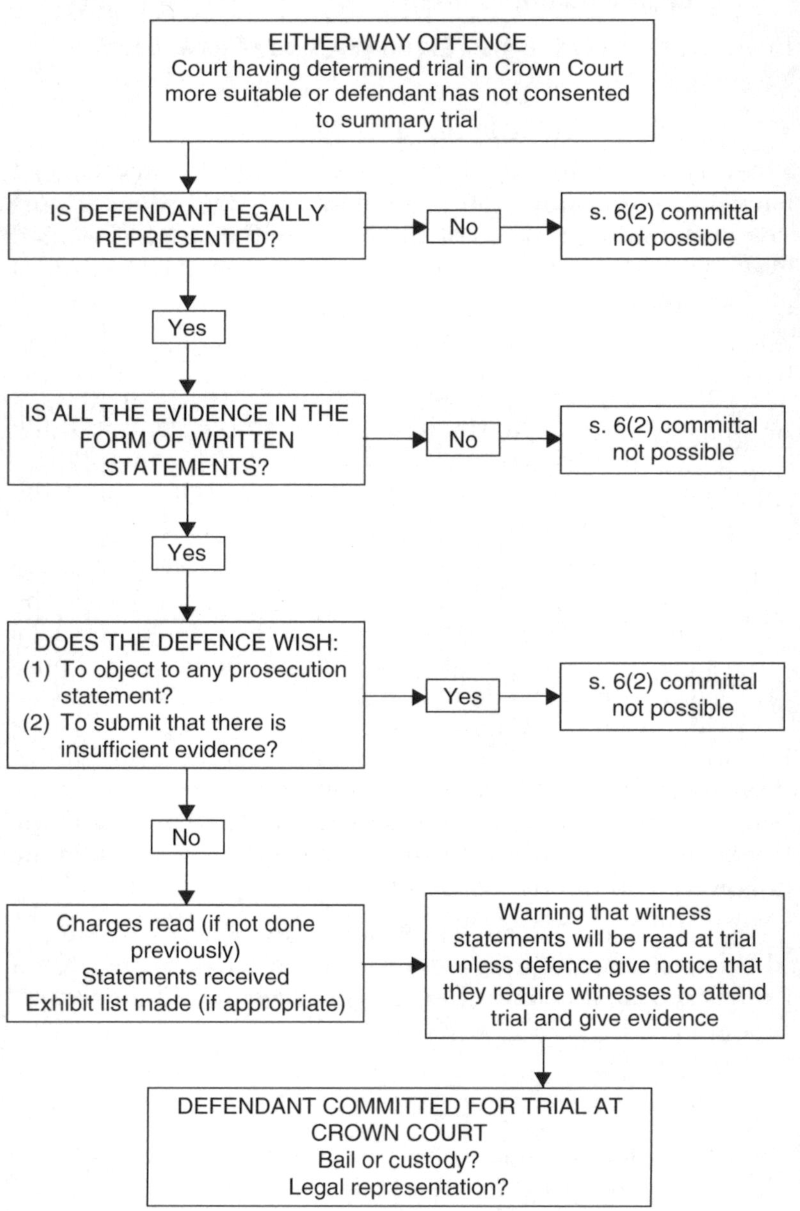

(d) the defence advocate does not wish to submit that the prosecution statements do not disclose a case against the defendant.

In effect, this form of committal takes place as a result of the agreement of both prosecution and defence (see Diagram C).

The "read through" committal

This form of committal arises as a result of the defence, having been served with copies of the prosecution witness statements, saying that the statements do not disclose a case for the defendant to answer.

In that situation, at the appropriate court hearing, the prosecution will produce the statements and they will either be read aloud or summarised for the magistrates after the prosecutor has explained what the case is about. After that, the defendant's advocate will make his submission that the statements do not disclose a case against the defendant (sometimes referred to as a "*prima facie*" case). The prosecution is entitled to respond to the submission.

If the submission is successful, the defendant will be discharged and, if he is not held for any other purpose, he will be free to leave. If the submission is unsuccessful, the defendant will be committed for trial in the Crown Court (see Diagram D overleaf).

In both types of committal, the magistrates must inform the defendant that the statements which have been produced before the court will be read out during his trial at the Crown Court instead of the witnesses attending to give evidence, unless the defendant gives notice to the prosecution and the Crown Court that he wishes the witnesses to attend.

The magistrates will then commit the defendant to the Crown Court for trial, specifying the date on which the defendant will first appear there, and will commit him either on bail or in custody.

Diagram D – Committal for trial: MCA 1980, s. 6(1) (consideration of the evidence)

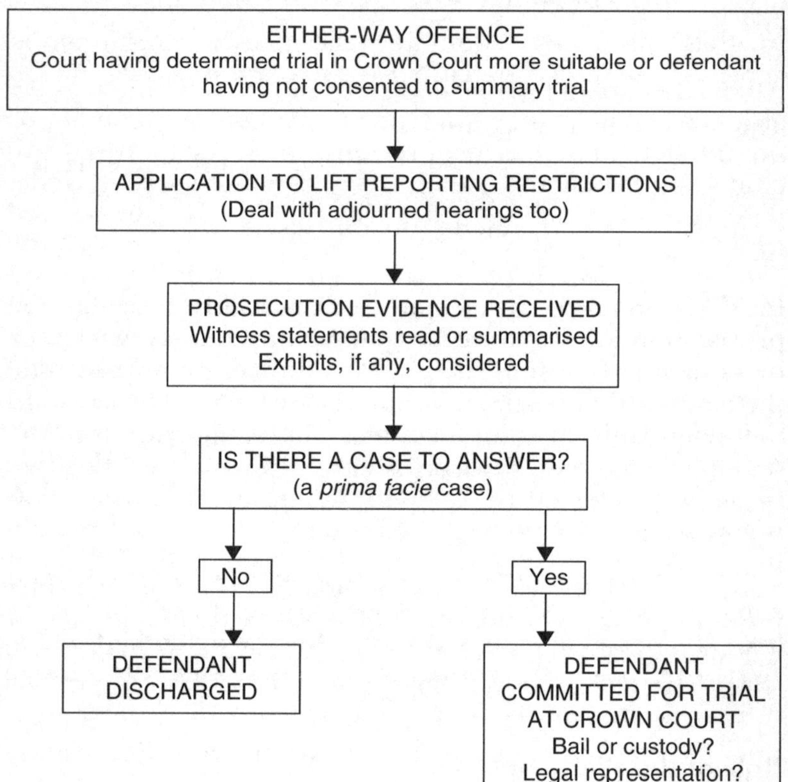

Chapter 14

SENTENCING ADULT OFFENDERS

After a defendant has pleaded guilty or has been found guilty after a trial, the prosecutor will inform the court whether or not the defendant has any previous convictions. If there are convictions, these will usually have been listed and, once the defendant or his advocate has seen the list, it will be handed to the magistrates for their consideration. Occasionally, the prosecution will provide the court with other relevant information about the defendant. It is at this stage that the prosecution will ask the magistrates to award costs against the defendant in favour of the prosecution and will usually state the amount that is asked for and may ask the court to award compensation to a defendant's victim. Thereafter, the defendant or his advocate will address the court in mitigation, bringing to the court's attention the personal details of the defendant's situation such as income and expenditure, job history, family matters, etc., and often suggesting the type or category of sentence he would ask the court to consider imposing. Either the court passes sentence there and then or adjourns for any reports it considers are necessary in the form of a pre-sentence report from the Probation Service or medical or psychiatric reports or any other report it may specify.

Role of the chairman

The chairman represents all three justices and passes sentence on behalf of them and should not pronounce any matter which they have not considered or approved. It is not a time for homily but rather a time for careful and considered delivery and explanation of the sentence that is passed, giving reasons as required by statutory provisions or generally. Whilst a court does not have to vindicate its sentence, the defendant and the general public must understand what the sentence is and what it involves and what may happen in the event of any breach by the defendant of any terms or requirements of the sentence. Nothing sounds more foolish than an ill-thought out, ill-delivered stricture. In adjourning the proceedings for a pre-sentence report, the chairman must be careful in what he says and not give the defendant the expectation of any particular sentence. In all probability, the magistrates then sitting will not be the ones passing sentence at the next hearing and the chairman should not tie the hands of the sentencing Bench. Therefore, to ensure that a defendant is not misled or given a false expectation of a particluar sentence, the chairman, when adjourning the case for a pre-sentence report, will say something to the effect that all sentencing options remain open.

The sentencing structure

The Criminal Justice Act 1991 introduced four levels of sentencing:

(1) Discharges.

(2) Fines.

(3) Community penalties.

(4) Custodial sentences (including committal to the Crown Court for sentence).

It is the seriousness of the offence, the character and circumstances of the defendant and the maximum penalty prescribed for the offence by Parliament that determines the "appropriate" sentence for a particular defendant.

The first matter that the magistrates need to know about the offence is the maximum penalty it carries. For example, it would appear foolish for a court to say in respect of an offence of driving a motor vehicle without insurance cover that it had a custodial sentence in mind when the statute creating the offence provides only for a fine, discretionary disqualification and penalty points. Thereafter, the court needs to consider what it wishes to achieve by a particular sentence - matters such as punishment, rehabilitation, compensation for a victim or no punishment at all for a technical offence - and to take into account those matters to lead to the appropriate sentence.

Credit for pleading guilty

When a court has determined the seriousness of the offence, it is in a position to say what it considers the appropriate sentence. The seriousness will be determined on the facts of the offence and any mitigation that may be adduced on behalf of the defendant. There is nothing to prevent a court from taking into account any matters which, in the court's opinion, are relevant in mitigating a sentence. Further, where the defendant has pleaded guilty, the court has power to give credit for that plea and reduce the sentence. The defendant who pleads guilty saves a great deal of time, spares witnesses and saves cost. When a court does give credit in this way, the magistrates must announce that fact when passing sentence.

Discharges

Absolute discharge

When, taking all relevant facts and matters into consideration, the magistrates do not think it appropriate to punish the offender in any way, they may impose on the defendant an absolute discharge which simply means that the defendant has been convicted of an offence and no other sentence is imposed.

For example, if a learner driver properly under supervision of a qualified driver affixes "L" plates both to the front and rear of his vehicle and, unknown to him, one of the "L" plates drops off during the course of his journey, in the event of a prosecution for failing to comply with that condition of his provisional driving licence, the court may well consider the matter is adequately dealt with by an absolute discharge as there is, effectively, no culpability on the part of the defendant.

Conditional discharge

The prerequisites for an absolute discharge are the same for a conditional discharge but here the defendant is discharged subject to the condition that he does not commit another offence during the period specified by the court. That period may not exceed three years. Should the defendant be convicted of an offence committed during that period, he will be liable to be punished for that offence and, additionally, for the offence in respect of which he was conditionally discharged.

Fines

A fine is the most-used sentence in a Magistrates' Court, particularly in cases of television and vehicle excise licence evasion and the majority of motoring offences.

The amount of a fine is limited by the maximum fine prescribed for the offence, the seriousness of the offence and the means of the offender. The maximum fine for an offence is ascertained by reference to the "standard scale" of fines, each offence having been assigned to a level on the scale by the statute creating the offence.

The standard scale is currently:

	Maximum fine
Level 1	£ 200
Level 2	£ 500
Level 3	£1,000
Level 4	£2,500
Level 5	£5,000

The maximum fine for an either-way offence is £5,000.

In assessing the seriousness of an offence, the court must take account of all relevant information about the circumstances of the offence, any aggravating factors and any factors advanced in mitigation, if appropriate.

The court should ask the defendant or his advocate for details of the defendant's means or order the defendant to complete a means statement form setting out all details of his income and expenditure.

Where fines are imposed for two or more offences, the court must bear in mind the "totality" principle, namely the overall culpability of the defendant in respect of the offences and then apportion fines accordingly. Where there are two or more offences, some Benches may deal with them by fixing on an overall sum, imposing that sum on one of the offences and marking the others "no separate penalty".

When a fine is imposed, payment should be made immediately. This is seldom the case, however, and the court, considering the defendant's means, may allow time for payment, for example 14 or 28 days, or order payment by weekly or monthly instalments. Ordinarily, any fine(s) imposed should be capable of payment within a year.

It is important that magistrates consider all these matters in detail, particularly the means aspect, as otherwise today's imposition may be tomorrow's enforcement problem.

If the court allows time for payment, either by instalments or within a specified period, it may fix a date on which the defendant must return to court for an inquiry into his means if payment has not been made in accordance with the terms set by the court.

If the court requires immediate payment and the defendant is unable to pay, the following powers may be exercised by the court:

Search

The court may order the defendant to be searched. Any money found as a result may, unless the court otherwise directs, be applied towards payment of the fine. Any balance must be repaid to the defendant. If the court is satisfied that any money found during the search does not belong to the defendant, it cannot be applied to payment; if the court considers that the loss of money found would be more injurious to the defendant's family than would be his detention, the court need not apply the money to payment of the fine.

Local detention for one day

In default of payment, a defendant may be ordered to be detained at the courthouse or in a police station until such hour as the court directs but not later than 8 p.m. on the day on which the order is made. In determining that time element, the court must not deprive the defendant of the opportunity of returning home at a reasonable time.

The order may be made, for example, where a defendant charged with drunkenness, who has been detained in custody overnight pending appearance before the court, pleads guilty. The court may regard the detention as sufficient punishment of the offence and order the payment of a fine with an alternative of one day's detention which discharges payment of the fine.

Transfer of fine order

If at the time of sentence a defendant resides in the jurisdiction of some other Magistrates' Court, the sentencing court may make a transfer of fine order to that other court which has the effect of transferring all powers of enforcement to that court. Thereafter, the sentencing court has no further jurisdiction in the matter.

Attachment of earnings order

An attachment of earnings order may be made on the application of a defendant who is in regular employment. Once made, the order is directed to the defendant's employer who is then required to deduct money from the defendant's salary and send it to the court in payment of the fine. The amount that is to be deducted each week or each month is specified by the court (the "normal deduction rate"). The court will also set an amount (the "protected earnings rate") that the defendant is allowed to receive by way of salary before any deductions are made. If the defendant's salary exceeds the protected earnings rate, the weekly or monthly deduction is to be made from the excess. If his salary in any particular week or month is less than the protected earnings rate, no deduction can be made.

Distress warrant

A distress warrant is authority for a police officer or some other authorised person, usually a bailiff, to enter the defendant's home or premises and seize property belonging to him, sell it at auction and pay the proceeds into the court in part-payment or settlement of the fine. Any property belonging to the defendant may be taken, save for his clothing and bedding and his tools, books, vehicle or equipment that he personally needs to use in his employment, business or vocation. If the money raised by sale of the property is only sufficient to pay the costs and charges incurred in executing the distress warrant, the fine remains outstanding and the court will consider other methods of enforcement.

Money payment supervision order

The court may order a defendant to be placed under the supervision of such a person as the court may from time to time appoint for the purpose of payment of a fine. The object is to advise the defendant and induce payment to avoid being sent to prison. The order remains in force until the fine has been paid but the court may revoke the order if it considers it appropriate to do so. Other alternative enforcement action cannot be taken while the order is in force and, if the court is considering some other action, it must obtain from the supervisor an oral or written report on the defendant's conduct and means while under supervision.

Committal to prison

The court may commit the defendant to prison if, having required immediate payment of the fine, the defendant does not make payment. This power is limited to three situations:

(a) where the offence is imprisonable and the defendant appears to have sufficient means to pay forthwith; or

(b) where the defendant appears unlikely to remain long enough at an address to enable enforcement by other methods; or

(c) where the defendant on that occasion is sentenced to immediate imprisonment for that or another offence or he is already serving a custodial sentence.

The court has power, however, to suspend the issue of the warrant of commitment to prison on such terms and conditions of payment as it thinks fit, ordering payment within a specified period or by instalments.

Compensation

If, as a result of a crime of which the defendant has been convicted, a person (the "victim") has suffered any loss or damage, the court must consider ordering the defendant to pay compensation to the victim in respect of the loss or damage.

The maximum amount of compensation that may be ordered in respect of an offence is £5,000. The court has to consider the defendant's means when an order is to be made and any compensation order is enforceable in the same manner as a fine.

While the prosecutor will often ask the magistrates to award compensation, the magistrates must consider making an order in any case where compensation arises, whether or not the prosecutor makes an application. If the magistrates do not order the defendant to pay compensation, they must state their reasons for that decision in open court.

Compensation may be ordered as an ancillary to any sentence passed by the court or it may be ordered as a sentence in itself.

Costs

On conviction of an offence, the prosecutor will ordinarily ask the court to consider ordering the defendant to pay the costs of the prosecution and will state a sum which the prosecution thinks is appropriate. The court has a discretion to order the costs in the sum that is mentioned or a lesser amount. Any award of costs is subject to the means of the defendant and the ability to pay.

The order to pay costs is always an order which is ancillary to the sentence passed on the defendant.

Community sentences

The community sentences the court may impose are:

(i) community rehabilitation order;

(ii) community punishment order;

(iii) community punishment and rehabilitation order;

(iv) curfew order;

(v) attendance centre order;

(vi) drug treatment and testing order.

Community rehabilitation order

This order replaces what was formerly known as a probation order. It may be made on conviction for an offence when the court considers that supervision of the defendant by a probation officer is desirable in the interests of:

(a) the defendant's rehabilitation; or

(b) protecting the public from harm or preventing the commission of further offences.

The order may be made for not less than six months nor more than three years.

The requirements of the order are that the defendant keeps in touch with his supervisor and complies with the supervisor's instructions and notifies him of any change of address. Other conditions, if appropriate, can be ordered, such as residence, medical treatment and participating in specified activities.

Community punishment order

This order was formerly known as a community service order and it can only be made in respect of an offence which is punishable by imprisonment.

The order involves the defendant doing unpaid work in the community under the supervision of the probation service. The number of hours to be worked will be specified by the magistrates, not being less than 40 nor more than 240. The further requirements are that the defendant keeps in touch with the relevant probation officer and notifies him of any change of address.

Community punishment and rehabilitation order

This order was formerly known as a combination order and it combines both supervision and work in the community. It can only be made in respect of an offence which is punishable by imprisonment. The order requires the defendant to be under supervision for a specified period of not less than 12 months nor more than three years and to perform unpaid work for not less than 40 hours nor more than 100 hours.

Curfew order

This order requires a defendant to remain at a specified place or places for specified periods. These:

(a) may be different places or different times for different days;

(b) periods may not fall outside a limit of six months beginning with the day on which the order is made; and

(c) may not be for periods of less than two hours nor more than 12 hours in any one day.

It is possible to secure the electronic monitoring of the

defendant's whereabouts during the curfew periods (commonly described as "tagging"), provided arrangements are available in the area in which the place(s) are and the court is satisfied that the necessary provision can be made.

As far as practicable, a curfew order must avoid any conflict with the defendant's religious beliefs or with the requirements of any other community orders to which he is subject and any interference with the times, if any, at which he normally works or attends school or other education establishments.

Attendance centre order

This order may be made when a defendant has been convicted of an offence which is punishable by imprisonment. The main aim of the order is to encourage defendants to make more constructive use of their leisure time in a structured environment.

The court is required to specify the number of hours for which the defendant is to attend, from a minimum of 12 hours to a maximum of 36.

Drug treatment and testing order

This order is designed to reduce the amount of crime which is attributable to drug misuse by reducing or eliminating the defendant's misuse of drugs. The order may only be made when the magistrates are satisfied that the defendant is dependent on or has a propensity to misuse drugs and that those matters may be susceptible to treatment. The order may be made for a minimum period of six months and a maximum period of three years.

The order involves the defendant complying with a drug testing regime operated by the probation service. The court will review the order at specific periods of not less than one month. The reviews are to be in open court with the defendant present. If the court is satisfied that the defendant is complying with the order and making good progress, subsequent reviews can be made without a specific court hearing and with the defendant's presence being excused.

The order cannot be made unless the offender has expressed his willingness to comply with its terms.

Preconditions for a community sentence

The magistrates cannot pass a community sentence unless they are of the opinion that the offence, or the combination of the offence and one or more offences associated with it, is serious enough for a community sentence. An "associated" offence is an offence of which the defendant is convicted and for which he is to be sentenced at the same time as he is to be sentenced for the other offence, or it is an offence which the defendant has admitted and asks that it be taken into consideration by the magistrates when they pass sentence in respect of the other offence.

Order suitable for the defendant

If the magistrates pass a community sentence, the particular order or orders must be such that they consider the most suitable for the defendant and the restriction placed on the defendant's liberty by the order(s) must be such as the magistrates consider to be commensurate with the seriousness of the offence(s). For those purposes, the magistrates must take into account all such information about the circumstances of the offence(s) as is available, including aggravating or mitigating factors, and any information about the offender that is available.

For the purpose of forming an opinion as to the suitability of the defendant for a community rehabilitation order, community punishment order, community punishment and rehabilitation order, or drug treatment and testing order, the magistrates must, unless they consider that it is not necessary to do so, obtain and consider a written pre-sentence report from a probation officer containing information about the defendant's suitability for any of those orders.

When the magistrates request a pre-sentence report, the proceedings will have to be adjourned for a maximum of three weeks if the defendant is remanded in custody or four weeks if on bail. If, however, the magistrates are considering a community rehabilitation order or a community punishment order, they may, instead of adjourning the proceedings to another date for the purposes of obtaining a pre-sentence report, put the case back during the course of the proceedings and request a probation officer to make a written report specifically as to the defendant's suitability for one or other of those orders – a "specific sentence report".

It must be emphasised that, if magistrates adjourn the proceedings for a pre-sentence report, the appropriate course is to request a report that considers all of the court's sentencing powers. Otherwise, if a report is requested for the consideration of community penalties only, that will create an expectation in the defendant's mind that a community sentence will be made if the recommendation by the maker of the report is favourable and will restrict the sentencing court to passing a community sentence. All sentencing options should be kept open.

Custodial sentences

The custodial sentences which may be passed by a Magistrates' Court are:

(i) detention in a Young Offenders' Institution for defendants aged 18 but under 21; or

(ii) imprisonment for defendants aged 21 or over.

Qualification for a custodial sentence

For a defendant to qualify for a custodial sentence, the magistrates must be of the opinion that the offence or the offence and one or more offences associated with it is so serious that only a custodial sentence can be justified for it or, if the offence is a violent or sexual offence, that only a custodial sentence would be adequate to protect the public from serious harm from him.

An offence is "so serious" if it is the kind of offence which would make right-thinking members of the public, knowing all the facts, feel that justice had not been done by the passing of any sentence other than a custodial one. A "sexual offence" is defined by including certain offences under the Sexual Offences Act 1956 and other statutes. Whether an offence is a "violent offence" is a question of fact in each case, dependent on the facts of the particular incident rather than the category of offence.

Preconditions for a custodial sentence

Before a custodial sentence can be considered and in order to form an opinion on the defendant's qualification for a custodial sentence, the magistrates must obtain a pre-sentence report, unless they are of the opinion that it is unnecessary to do so.

Defendant not legally represented

A court must not pass a custodial sentence - imprisonment or detention - on a defendant who has not previously been sentenced to a custodial sentence if he has not had an advocate to represent him after being found guilty, unless the defendant applied to the court for a legal representation order and his application was refused or, on being informed of his right to apply for such an order, he failed or refused to do so.

Length of sentence

The maximum period of detention or imprisonment for an offence is specified in the statute creating the offence and, subject to any lesser period specified by the statute, the maximum term will not be more than six months for any one offence. Where, however, the defendant has been convicted of two or more either-way offences, the maximum term will be 12 months.

Suspended imprisonment

A term of imprisonment imposed by the court may be suspended for a term of not less than one year nor more than two years.

The effect of a suspended sentence is that the term of imprisonment will not take effect unless the defendant commits another offence punishable by imprisonment within the period of suspension specified by the court.

A suspended sentence cannot be imposed unless the magistrates are of the opinion that (i) the case is one in which a sentence of immediate imprisonment would have been appropriate even without the power to suspend, and (ii) that suspension can be justified by the exceptional circumstances of the case, which relates to the offence or the defendant. "Exceptional circumstances" are not defined: they will depend on the facts of each case. However, the higher courts have said that, either on their own or in combination, good character, youth and an early plea of guilty are not exceptional circumstances justifying suspension.

Breach of suspended sentence

Where a defendant is convicted of a further offence punishable by imprisonment committed during the operational period of a suspended sentence, the court must consider the suspended sentence and deal with it in one of four ways:

(a) order it to take effect; or

(b) order it to take effect with the substitution of a lesser term of imprisonment; or

(c) vary the original sentence by extending the operational period to expire not later than two years from the date of the variation; or

(d) make no order.

Detention of young offenders

Defendants aged 18 but under 21 years convicted of an offence punishable in the case of a person over 21 with imprisonment may, if the pre-conditions for a sentence of imprisonment are made out, be sent to detention in a Young Offenders' Institution. The maximum term of detention is the same as the maximum sentence of imprisonment. The minimum term is 21 days. If the defendant is convicted of two or more either-way offences, the maximum term is 12 months.

Deferment of sentence

Instead of passing sentence on a defendant immediately, the magistrates may defer passing sentence for a specified period up to a maximum of six months for the court to be able to have regard to:

(a) his conduct after conviction;

(b) the making by him of reparation for his offence where that is appropriate; and/or

(c) any change in his circumstances.

The magistrates must be satisfied that it is in the interests of justice to defer sentence and the defendant must agree to that course. The superior courts have said that the power to defer was intended for cases such as where recent developments have shown that the defendant may be settling down; or where the defendant has already shown signs of amending his life such as holding down a job and a change in his attitude.

Committal to the Crown Court for sentence

Where the defendant has been convicted of one or more either-way offences and the magistrates consider it appropriate in all the circumstances of the offence(s) and of the defendant, they may commit the defendant to the Crown Court for sentence. The Crown Court will impose a sentence that it thinks is appropriate, which may be a heavier sentence than the magistrates can impose or a sentence which was within the magistrates' power to impose.

The effect of previous convictions

Previous convictions of a defendant may be taken into account by the sentencing court and make the offence more serious. However, the court should note when taking previous convictions into account that the defendant has already been punished for the offences giving rise to the previous convictions and should not punish the defendant a second time for those offences. Previous convictions may, however, reduce the impact of any mitigation that has been put before the court.

Sentencing guidelines

The superior courts have given guidance on sentencing for particular offences and the Magistrates' Association has published sentencing guidelines for the vast majority of offences that come before the court. It is part of the legal adviser's duty to bring to the attention of the magistrates any guidance that has been given.

Homilies accompanying sentence should be avoided; they are unnecessary and rarely have any effect on a defendant. A defendant must not be punished additionally because, for example, his defence necessitated searching cross-examination of prosecution witnesses. Neither are there prizes for advocacy; nor should a defendant be penalised for any failings in his advocate. The defendant is an individual and, although the public must be protected and potential wrong-doers dissuaded from crime, sentence must be based on all the circumstances of the case before the court which have been admitted or proved. Magistrates must pass what they consider to be the appropriate sentence for the particular defendant based on proper principles and guidelines and ignore any adverse reaction by the media or their acquaintances.

Pre-sentence report

The pre-sentence report is prepared by the Probation Service. Its purpose is to provide a sentencing court with information about the defendant and the offence(s) he has pleaded guilty to or has been found guilty of committing so that the court has as much relevant information as possible to enable it to decide an appropriate sentence. National Standards require the report to contain:

(a) an assessment of the defendant's offending behaviour;

(b) an assessment of his risk to the public; and

(c) a clear and realistic indication of the action which can be taken by the court to reduce re-offending.

When adjourning a case for the purpose of obtaining a report, the magistrates should indicate:

(a) their preliminary view of the level of seriousness of the offence(s);

(b) the aim of the sentence; and

(c) any other issues they wish to be addressed in the report.

However, the magistrates must make it clearly and unequivocally understood to everyone in the court that the court which ultimately passes sentence is not bound by the preliminary indication of seriousness of the offence.

If the magistrates are contemplating a custodial sentence, or community rehabilitation order, a community punishment order, a community punishment and rehabilitation order or a drug treatment and testing order, they are required to obtain and consider a pre-sentence report before forming an opinion on the appropriate sentence, unless they consider that it is unnecessary to obtain a report. In forming that opinion, the magistrates are required to take into account all the available information about the circumstances of the offence and any associated offence(s), including any aggravating or mitigating factors and any information that is available about the defendant. Examples of when a court may consider a pre-sentence report is not necessary are where the offence is so serious that a custodial sentence is inevitable or where the defendant is already subject to a community sentence and the court considers that a further similar sentence is appropriate.

Where a case is adjourned for a pre-sentence report to be obtained, the report writer will be assisted by some initial indication of the magistrates' views of the seriousness of the offence subject to the caveat that the sentencing court will not be restricted to a particular sentence.

Specific sentence report

Whilst magistrates need not obtain a pre-sentence report where they consider it unnecessary to do so, it is good practice for them to obtain one. Where the magistrates are thinking in terms of a community punishment order or a community rehabilitation order, they can obtain a specific sentence report. Such a report has a similar purpose to the pre-sentence report but it is expedited and, where a community punishment order is under consideration, it will assess the defendant's suitability for that sentence and the availability of work under the order. The report will be available on the same day that it is requested, unless the probation officer considers that a pre-sentence report is necessary for any reasons he specifies. The value of a specific sentence report is that it speeds up the provision of information and allows the court to sentence without delay.

Mentally disordered offenders

Some offenders may be in need of psychiatric treatment. It may be appropriate in some cases for the magistrates to make a community rehabilitation order with a requirement to undergo psychiatric treatment; in other cases it may be appropriate for a hospital order to be made. Where a person is convicted of an offence punishable by imprisonment and preconditions are met, the magistrates have power to make a hospital order which is authority for a person's admission to, and detention in, a hospital specified in the order. It is also possible for the order to be made otherwise than on conviction.

Preconditions for a hospital order

Subject to the exception mentioned below, for a hospital order to be made the magistrates must be dealing with a person who has been convicted of an imprisonable offence and:

(a) they must be satisfied on the written or oral evidence of two medical practitioners, at least one of whom is approved for the provision of such evidence, that:

   (i) the person concerned is suffering from mental illness, psychopathic disorder, mental impairment or severe mental impairment of a nature or to a degree which makes it appropriate for him to be detained in a hospital for medical treatment; and

   (ii) in the case of psychopathic disorder or mental impairment, the treatment is likely to alleviate or prevent the deterioration of his condition;

(b) they must be satisfied that a place is available for him at a specified hospital and that arrangements have been made for his admission within 28 days; and

(c) in all the circumstances and having regard to other methods of dealing with him, the hospital order is the most suitable.

Hospital order otherwise than on conviction

If a person is before the court charged with an offence and the court would have the power to make a hospital order on conviction as he is a person who is suffering from mental illness or mental impairment, the magistrates may, if they are satisfied that he did the act or made the omission with which he is charged, make a hospital order without convicting him.

The order cannot be made when the person has been charged with an offence which is indictable only.

Chapter 15

MOTORING OFFENCES

A large part of a magistrate's work is spent dealing with motoring and road traffic offences. These offences are in the main summary offences and as such have to be dealt with by the Magistrates' Court. They range from matters such as parking in a restricted street, documentary offences such as driving without insurance cover, and defects in the motor vehicle such as bald tyres, through to driving without due care and attention and dangerous driving.

Whether a defendant pleads guilty or not guilty, the procedures to be followed are exactly the same as those for any other criminal offence dealt with by the court. The duties and responsibilities of the advocate are also the same.

Motoring offences arising out of accidents and those of driving without due care and attention can be difficult for magistrates to deal with because the incidents giving rise to them often happen quickly and unexpectedly, with the result that the drivers concerned and other witnesses gain only a fleeting and frequently imperfect impression of the events. It often happens that they are unable to give reliable details and distance, which is not a criticism but a reality because of all the circumstances pertaining at the relevant time and, on occasions, because of the passage of time between the incidents and the trial.

There is seldom a legal problem in the trial of road traffic offences and, in the vast majority of cases, the only issues for magistrates to determine are issues of fact, difficult as those can be. The crucial question for the magistrates in that situation is one of credibility of the witnesses – "who do I believe and why?"

In matters such as driving dangerously or without due care and attention, magistrates are often assisted by the prosecutor opening the case, setting out, for example, how it is suggested that a defendant's driving was at fault and in which respects the driving lacked due care and attention or was dangerous. Again, in opening, the prosecutor must mention only matters that will be supported or established by the evidence in the case.

Plans and sketches

It is not easy to give a verbal picture of a road and road markings; a witness may become incoherent when attempting to describe the scene of an accident. It is no longer the case that in virtually all dangerous driving and due care and attention cases an accurate, scaled plan of the road, etc. is prepared for the magistrates; in fact, the reverse is now true. However, police officers who attend the scene of an accident will often make, at the time, a sketch in their notebooks of the scene. If the sketch is accepted as a true representation, it can be produced as part of the evidence to which the magistrates may have regard. Witnesses may be invited to make a sketch which again, if accepted by both the prosecution and the defence, may be allowed in evidence. Nevertheless, sketches should be accepted with caution because of the fact they are what the name implies and are not an accurate, to scale, diagram.

Magistrates with local knowledge

On occasions, a magistrate has personal knowledge of the locality of an accident. Whilst a magistrate may rely on such knowledge, he should make that fact known to the parties but should be alert to the possibility that:

(a) his memory may not be accurate;

(b) his mental picture may not coincide with that of a colleague or the witness;

(c) the locality may have altered in some way; and

(d) he cannot be cross-examined as to the quality of his memory.

The Highway Code

Magistrates are reminded that the Highway Code has not the same force as a statutory provision or regulation. Failure to observe the Code does not, of itself, render a person liable to criminal proceedings. The fact that a motorist has not exactly obeyed the advice set out in the Code does not, alone, cause him to be convicted. However, a failure to observe the Code may be relied on by either party to the proceedings as tending to establish or negate any liability which is in question.

Sentencing road traffic offenders

Motoring offenders must be sentenced and the vast majority are dealt with by a fine, with or without an order for payment of an amount specified by the court as prosecution costs. When imposing a fine, magistrates must still have regard to the seriousness or otherwise of the offence and the means of the offender and any previous convictions. These provisions make magistrates, for good reason, discriminate between offenders and this is particularly important when dealing with motoring offenders in the sense that many Benches have their own guidelines for sentencing or employ those of the Magistrates' Association. These are no more than notional starting points which may go up or, more often, down in the light of the particular circumstances of the instant offence and the offender. The guidelines must never be seen as "the fine for this offence" nor as a fixed penalty. There is considerable difference between, say, a "weekend" motorist who shows a blatant disregard for speed limits and other road traffic matters and a person driving a lorry day after day in busy traffic conditions who inadvertently commits a road traffic offence.

Endorsement, penalty points and disqualification

The Road Traffic Offenders Act 1988 sets out the offences which carry an obligatory endorsement of the offender's driving licence. Every endorsable offence attracts penalty points, the number of points varying according to the particular offence, and discretionary disqualification. Some offences such as drink/driving offences and dangerous driving attract a mandatory period of disqualification of not less than one year. In prescribed circumstances, a second or subsequent drink/driving offence will carry a mandatory disqualification of not less than three years. Magistrates cannot be expected to memorise all of these matters and should consult the legal adviser appropriately.

"Totting" disqualification

Where a road traffic offender is convicted of endorsable offences committed within three years of one another, any penalty points ordered to be imposed in respect of those offences will be added together by the court dealing with the last of those offences. If the total is 12 points or more, the court is required to disqualify the offender from driving for a minimum period of six months – commonly referred to as "totting". The disqualification must be imposed unless the court finds "mitigating circumstances" which would justify the court in reducing the period of disqualification or not disqualifing at all. The disqualification is the result of repeated offending within a comparatively short period, whether or not the offences in themselves would justify disqualification.

"Mitigating circumstances" are not defined by the Act; the Act simply excludes from consideration any circumstances:

(a) that are alleged to make the offence not serious; or

(b) that show hardship which is short of "exceptional hardship"; or

(c) which have been taken into consideration on another occasion within the three years immediately preceding the latest convictions.

If the offender wishes to advance "mitigating circumstances", it is usual, but not mandatory, for the offender to give evidence on oath about those circumstances. It is important to note that "mitigating circumstances" relate to the offender and are not concerned with the gravity of the offence.

If the latest offence in the three-year period is one which carries a mandatory disqualification, that disqualification must be imposed and cannot be reduced by way of "mitigating circumstances".

"Special reasons"

A road traffic offender who is convicted of an offence for which his driving licence must be endorsed, or is one for which a mandatory period of disqualification must be imposed, may be able to adduce what are called "special reasons" for not endorsing his driving licence or imposing the mandatory disqualification. Special reasons (which are separate and distinct from the "mitigating circumstances" under "totting" and should not be confused with them) must fulfil four conditions, namely that the facts advanced:

(1) Must amount to mitigating or extenuating circumstances.

(2) Must not amount to a defence to the offence which has been charged.

(3) Must be directly connected with the commission of the offence.

(4) Must be matters which can properly be taken into account when imposing punishment.

Unlike mitigating circumstances which are relevant to the *offender*, the facts in a special reasons application must be "special" to the *offence*.

The majority of cases in which offenders seek to put forward special reasons relate to drink/drive offences (which carry a minimum of 12 months' disqualification). An example is that of a sudden medical emergency – an unexpected situation arising in which a person who has been drinking but not intending to drive is impelled to drive as a result. In such cases, the court is required to consider the whole circumstances of the case, including the nature and degree of the emergency which caused the offender to drive and, further:

(a) whether the emergency was sufficiently acute to justify the offender driving;

(b) whether there were alternative means of transport available, such as taxis or the emergency services;

(c) whether there were alternative means of dealing with the emergency;

(d) the manner of the offender's driving; and

(e) whether the offender otherwise acted reasonably and responsibly.

The mere fact that the circumstances disclose a special reason does not mean, of itself, that an offender is entitled, as a matter of course, to avoid disqualification. The court has to decide, in its discretion, whether to refrain from imposing the disqualification or to impose a shorter period of disqualification. The court's powers should only be exercised in clear and compelling circumstances.

Interim disqualification

Where a defendant has been convicted of an offence involving mandatory or discretionary disqualification and the magistrates:

(a) commit him to the Crown Court for sentence;

(b) remit him to another Magistrates' Court for sentence;

(c) defer passing sentence on him; or

(d) adjourn his case after conviction before dealing with him,

the magistrates may disqualify him from driving until such time as he is sentenced. It is not necessary for magistrates to specify a period of disqualification but, if the defendant is not sentenced before the expiry of six months from the date of the order, the order will cease to have effect. If the sentencing court imposes a disqualification, it will be reduced by the time during which the defendant was subject to the interim disqualification.

Rehabilitation courses for drink/drive offenders

Where the Secretary of State has provided for a scheme by which the periods of disqualification imposed on drink/driving offenders may be reduced by their attendance on courses, magistrates, at the time of sentence when the disqualification is imposed, have power to order that the period of disqualification be reduced if the offender satisfactorily completes a specified approved course.

The offender must have been convicted of:

(a) driving or being in charge of a motor vehicle when under the influence of drink or drugs;

(b) driving or being in charge of a motor vehicle with excess alcohol; or

(c) failing to provide a specimen for a laboratory test.

These offences carry a minimum mandatory disqualification of 12 months and the reduction period, if the course is satisfactorily completed, will not be less than three months and must not exceed one quarter of the unreduced period. The order cannot be made unless:

(a) the magistrates are satisfied that a course is available;

(b) the offender is aged 17 or more;

(c) the effect of the course is explained in ordinary language to the offender and he is informed of the fees he must pay and the necessity for payment of them before the course begins; and

(d) the offender agrees to the order being made.

Chapter 16

THE YOUTH COURT

Not far back in this country's criminal justice system, offenders could expect neither sympathy nor understanding from the courts, only retribution and punishment. Punishments were imaginative and sadistic in their cruelty, were disproportionately severe when measured against offences, and did not distinguish between men, women, young persons and children. Society, often as a result of a jury returning a perverse verdict - sometimes to ensure an offender was not sentenced to death for what might be regarded as minor offences - began to revolt against extremes of punishment. Thus it came to be accepted that the sex and age of an offender and the circumstances of the offence and the offender were matters that should affect sentence, and that juveniles, that is persons under the age of 18, should generally be treated in a different manner to adults. This led to the establishment of courts specifically to deal with juveniles - the Juvenile Court, now known as the Youth Court - and as a result it was accepted that juveniles, save in some exceptional circumstances, should be tried and dealt with in that court.

The court

A Youth Court must, wherever possible, be held in a different part of the building or courtroom from that of the (adult) Magistrates' Court. Where a specific courtroom is used as a Youth Court, it is usually designed so that its appearance is not as awe-inspiring as an adult courtroom. For example, there is no dock or witness box and the magistrates sit at a table on the same level as everyone else in the courtroom.

A Youth Court is a "closed" court in the sense that only members and officers of the court, parties to the particular case then being heard, their legal representatives, witnesses and *bona fide* members of the press may be present. Other persons who are authorised to be present are social workers, members of the Youth Offending Team and probation officers.

The magistrates

Only magistrates who are "specially qualified" to be members of the Youth Court panel may sit in the Youth Court. Those magistrates receive special training and are chosen by and from the magistrates who are assigned to sit in that Magistrates' Court area. Save in emergency or exceptional circumstances, the court should be comprised of three youth panel magistrates, at least one of whom is a male and one a female. One of them will also be a specially appointed chairman. A District Judge may sit as chairman with two justices but he is also empowered to sit alone.

Juveniles

Juveniles are:

(1) Children (those who are aged under 14).

(2) Young persons (those aged 14 and under 18).

If the precise age of a juvenile before the court is not known, the court will deem him to be the age he appears to be after the court has considered all the available evidence. A child under the age of 10 cannot be guilty of any criminal offence.

Reporting restrictions

Although *bona fide* members of the press may be present in court, there is a restriction on the matters which may be reported in the media. The name, address and school of the defendant or a juvenile witness must not be reported nor any details which would identify them, which includes a printed photograph. In prescribed circumstances, the court has power to lift the restrictions.

Criminal proceedings

The court must, in the case of a child or a young person under the age of 16, insist that the parent or guardian of that defendant is present in court unless it is unreasonable to do so. In the case of defendants who are 16 and 17 years old, the court has a discretion in that respect. If a parent refuses to attend, the court has the power to issue a warrant for his/her arrest.

A trial in the Youth Court follows the same procedure as in the adult court. The burden and standard of proof are the same, as are the duties of the advocates. In the main part, the rules of evidence are the same.

The principal aims of the Youth Court and the criminal youth justice system are to prevent a juvenile from reoffending and to have regard to his welfare. It is essential for the court to ensure that the juvenile understands the proceedings and the matter(s) with which he has been charged, with all things being explained to him in words he understands.

When giving evidence, every witness in the Youth Court takes a modified form of oath, "promising" rather than "swearing" to tell the truth.

The powers to adjourn Youth Court proceedings are the same as for the adult court but the powers of remand differ according to the age of the juvenile. The Bail Act provisions are the same in that, if a juvenile is not granted unconditional bail, exceptions and reasons have to be given. Where the juvenile is aged 17, the adult remand powers apply.

Powers of remand: juveniles under 17 years of age

1. 10-11 year olds, male and female

(a) bail, with or without conditions; or

(b) remand to local authority accommodation. After consultation with the local authority, the court may require the juvenile so remanded to comply with conditions analogous to bail conditions. The court may formally order the local authority to ensure that the juvenile complies with the conditions; or

(c) where the juvenile has been remanded to local authority accommodation, the authority may apply to the court for a "secure accommodation order", provided it can satisfy strict conditions that:

(i) the juvenile has a history of absconding and is likely to abscond from any other description of accommodation and that, if he absconded, he is likely to suffer significant harm; or

(ii) that if he is kept in any other description of

accommodation, he is likely to injure himself or other persons.

2. 12-14 year olds, male and female, and 15-16 year old females

The powers of remand are the same as at (a) above, together with the further power of the court itself to remand the juvenile into local authority secure accommodation if the following criteria are met:

(a) that the juvenile is charged with or has been convicted of a violent or sexual offence, or an offence punishable in the case of an adult with imprisonment for 14 years or more;

or

(b) the juvenile has a recent history of absconding while remanded into local authority accommodation and is charged with or has been convicted of an imprisonable offence alleged to be, or found to have been, committed while so remanded;

and in either case

(c) the court is of the opinion that only remanding the juvenile to local authority secure accommodation will be adequate to protect the public from serious harm from him or her.

Such a remand is a formal requirement that the local authority keep the juvenile in secure accommodation. The court must, however, consult the local authority before such a remand can be ordered so that the magistrates may be assisted with any information in making the appropriate decision. When ordering such a remand, the magistrates must state in open court why they are of the opinion that a remand into secure accommodation is appropriate to protect the public from serious harm from the juvenile and must explain the same to the juvenile.

3. 15-16 year old males

The powers are the same as 1(a)-(c) and 2(a)-(c) above.

There is an additional power of remand. If the juvenile satisfies the criteria at 2(a)-(c) above, he may be remanded into local authority secure accommodation if the court declares him to be "vulnerable" and provided that secure accommodation has been made available for him. In declaring the juvenile to be vulnerable, the court is recognising that, because of his physical or emotional immaturity or because of his propensity to harm himself, he should not be remanded to prison accommodation.

The magistrates must state in open court that they are of the opinion that a secure accommodation remand or a remand to prison accommodation is necessary to protect the public from serious harm from the juvenile, or that he is vulnerable, and must explain the same to him.

Committal to the Crown Court for trial

All alleged offences against juveniles must be tried in the Youth Court, with the exception of the following:

(1) Homicide.

(2) Where the offence is punishable by 14 years' imprisonment or more in the case of an adult, or is an indecent assault, or is an offence of causing death as a result of a road traffic offence and the juvenile is aged 10 (or, in the case of the road traffic offence, is aged 14) but not more than 17, he must be committed for trial if the magistrates are of the opinion that, in the event of his being found guilty of the offence, he should be detained for a period longer than two years.

(If a juvenile is jointly charged with an adult in respect of an either-way offence not being one of the above offences, he must be tried in the Magistrates's Court or Youth Court, unless the court considers it necessary in the interests of justice for him to be committed for trial at the Crown Court with the adult.)

Remission to other courts

If a juvenile jointly charged with an adult is not committed for trial in the Crown Court and he admits the charge(s) against him, the Magistrates' Court has very limited powers of sentence and it would be more likely than not that the court would remit him to a Youth Court for sentence. The remittal will be to a Youth Court acting for the area in which he lives. If he denies the charge(s), he would normally be remanded to appear before the Youth Court for his trial to take place there.

The adult court powers of sentence in respect of a juvenile are:

(a) absolute discharge;

(b) conditional discharge;

(c) fine (maximum for a child is £250; maximum for a young person is £1,000).

Cost, compensation, disqualification and endorsement can be imposed as ancillary orders.

Where a juvenile attains 18 years of age before sentence in the Youth Court, he may be remitted to the adult court to be sentenced.

Chapter 17

LICENSING

One of the more important administrative duties of magistrates is the control and licensing of the sale of intoxicating liquor and the control of betting and gaming. These duties are undertaken not by the Magistrates' Court but by the licensing committee and the betting and gaming licensing committee. These committees are elected at the Magistrates' Annual General Meeting (which is held in October each year) from among the magistrates who serve in the court's area.

The licensing committee

With the exception of theatres, passenger aircraft, railway passenger trains and some other minor cases, intoxicating liquor can only be sold by retail by the holder of a justices' licence and only at the premises specified in the licence. To do otherwise than under the authority of such a licence is a criminal offence. Applications for the grant of such licences are made to the court's licensing committee, either at the annual licensing meeting of the committee (which is held during the first fortnight in February each year) or at one of the committee's transfer sessions (of which there must not be less than four in each year).

The licensing committee must not be less than five in number nor more than 20. The quorum for a licensing meeting or a transfer session is three. Usually, three or five members of the committee sit on those occasions.

The functions of the committee are exercised at licensing sessions which comprise:

(1) The general annual licensing meeting held in the first fortnight of February.

(2) Not less than four transfer sessions thereafter in every year.

Justices' licences

At the licensing sessions, the committee hears and decides amongst other things applications for:

(1) The grant of licences and the renewal, revocation, transfer and removal of licences already in existence.

(2) Consent to alterations to licensed premises.

(3) Certificates for extending the hours licensed premises may be open for matters such as serving food with alcohol, music and dancing.

(4) Occasional permissions (the authority to sell intoxicating liquor at some charitable or similar event).

A justices' licence authorises the sale by retail of intoxicating liquor and is either:

(a) an *on-licence* which authorises the sale for consumption on or off the premises for which the licence is granted of:

(i) all descriptions of intoxicating liquor; or

(ii) beer, cider and wine only; or

(iii) beer and cider only; or

(iv) wine only;

or

(b) an *off-licence* which authorises the sale for consumption off the premises of:

(i) all descriptions of intoxicating liquor; or

(ii) beer, cider and wine only.

The committee is also responsible for the grant of restaurant licences. A restaurant licence may be granted:

(a) for premises which are structurally adapted and *bona fide* used, or are intended to be used, for the purpose of habitually providing the customary main meal at midday or in the evening, or both, for the accommodation of persons frequenting the premises; and

(b) subject to the condition that intoxicating liquor shall not be sold or supplied on the premises otherwise than to persons taking table meals there and for consumption by such persons as an ancillary to their meal.

A licence may be granted to any person who is not disqualified under the provisions of the Licensing Act 1964 or any other legal provision and whom the committee think is a fit and proper person to hold a licence. When considering whether an applicant is a "fit and proper person", the committee is not confined to an inquiry as to his character; his health, temper and disposition may be considered, as may his security of tenure of the licensed premises.

With few exceptions, a justices' licence has effect from the time it is granted until the expiry of the current licensing period, that is, a period of three years beginning on 5 April 2002 or any triennial of that date.

Permitted hours

The permitted hours in licensed premises during which intoxicating liquor can be supplied and consumed vary according to the type of licence that has been granted, the purpose for which it has been granted and any conditions attached to it.

Procedure before the committee

No statute or regulations specify the procedure during a licence application which the committee must follow but the committee must, of course, comply with all pertinent legislation and have regard to the decisions of higher courts on points of law. Thereafter, the committee bases its decisions on what it considers relevant in the particular circumstances. It is important to remember that the committee is not a court as such and is therefore not bound by the rules of evidence and procedures of the Magistrates' Court, nor the standards of proof. Hearsay evidence is often given and how much reliance the committee puts on this will depend on the circumstances of the application and the nature of that evidence.

Before an application is made to the committee at one of its licensing sessions, there is a strict statutory procedure which an applicant must follow, including a requirement to display a notice at the premises in question of the applicant's intention to apply for a licence and advertising that fact in a newspaper which circulates in the local area. At the hearing other interested parties, such as local residents, licensed victuallers' associations and the police may be heard in opposition to the application or otherwise. Most committees follow a procedure along the following lines:

(1) The applicant or his advocate outlines the application.

(2) The applicant and his witnesses, if any, give evidence and may be cross-examined by any objectors or their advocates.

(3) Any objectors, in turn, may state their objections usually, but not necessarily, on oath or affirmation. Objectors may be cross-examined by the applicant or his advocate.

(4) The applicant or his advocate may address the committee in conclusion.

The decision of the committee on the application may be by majority but, when the committee members are equally divided, the chairman, unlike the chairman in a Magistrates' Court, has a casting vote.

Appeals from committee decisions are heard in the Crown Court, usually by a Circuit Judge sitting with two committee members who were not party to the decision which is being appealed and two members of another area's committee.

There is much licensing law, some of which is complex and not easily understood and the procedures to be followed by an applicant must be strictly enforced. As in the Magistrates' Court, the committee will have a legal adviser throughout the proceedings who has the same duties and responsibilities.

Protection orders

A person who intends to apply to a licensing committee for the transfer to him of a justices' licence may apply to the Magistrates' Court for the area in which the licensed premises are situated for what is called a protection order which would permit him to sell intoxicating liquor pending the transfer to him of the justices' licence. If the magistrates are satisfied that he is a person to whom the licensing justices could transfer the licence, they are able to grant such an order.

An application for this order is made, for example, when the holder of a justices' licence has died; or the licensee has sold the licensed premises to the applicant and has nothing more to do with the premises; or where the licensee has become a disqualified person for holding a justices' licence.

Occasional licence

An occasional licence is granted by the Magistrates' Court to the holder of a justices' on-licence to allow him to sell intoxicating liquor, to which his on-licence extends, at such a place other than the premises for which the on-licence has been granted and during such period not exceeding three weeks at one time, and between such hours, as the court specifies.

An occasional licence may be granted, for example, where the licensee is asked to sell intoxicating liquor at a wedding reception held in unlicensed premises, such as a church or community hall, or at sporting events such as a village cricket match or a regatta.

Occasional permission

The licensing justices may grant an officer of an eligible organisation or a branch of it an "occasional permission" to sell intoxicating liquor during a period not exceeding 24 hours at a function held by the organisation or branch in connection with its activities. An "eligible organisation" is one carried for purposes other than personal gain, such as a charitable organisation. It should not be confused with an occasional licence.

The betting and gaming licensing committee

This committee is responsible for the grant and renewal of bookmakers' permits, betting agency permits and betting office licences. The number of justices who comprise the committee must not be less than five nor more than 15. Under the name of the gaming committee, it is also responsible for the grant, renewal, cancellation and transfer of gaming licences.

The committees are required to deal with these matters in the months of January, April, July and October. Further sessions may be held as necessary.

A *betting office licence* may be granted for premises to be used for the effecting of betting transactions with, or through, the licence holder or his servants or agents. The legislation specifies who may apply for such a licence.

A *bookmaker's permit* may be granted to a person to act as a bookmaker on his own account. A "bookmaker" means a person, otherwise than the Totalisator Board, who:

(a) carries on the business of receiving or negotiating bets or conducts pool betting operations, either on his own account or as servant or agent to another person; or

(b) who holds himself out or permits himself to be held out, by way of business, as a person who receives or negotiates bets or conducts such operations.

With one exception, any applicant for a betting office licence must be the holder or a bookmaker's permit or a betting agency permit which itself authorises the holder to be an applicant for a betting office licence.

Applicants for licences and permits must follow a very complex procedure, all of which is governed by specified time periods.

"Gaming" is defined as the playing of a game of chance for winnings in money or money's worth, whether any person playing the game is at risk of losing money or money's worth or not, and the control of gaming is to a large extent governed by the amount of commercial profit which is likely to be made from it, the most notable examples of which are casino games and bingo.

Any applicant for a gaming licence must have a certificate issued by the Gaming Board of Great Britain consenting to his application to the committee for a licence and specifying the period within which the application must be made. The reason for this is that the Board has a duty to keep under review the extent and character of gaming and, particularly, keep under review the extent, character and location of gaming facilities.

Thereafter, there is another inflexible procedure the applicant has to follow before his application can be heard by the committee.

Both in betting and gaming applications, there are strict grounds on which the committees may grant or refuse applications and appeals against the committees' decisions are heard by the Crown Court.

Chapter 18

THE FAMILY PROCEEDINGS COURT

Only magistrates who have been appointed to the Family Proceedings panel may sit in the Family Proceedings Court. Appointments to the panel are made by the magistrates at their annual meeting in October and appointments are for periods of three years. The panel will have specially trained chairmen and, except in emergency or unforeseen circumstances, one of them will preside in court. So far as is practicable, the court must include a male and a female.

Jurisdiction

The jurisdiction of the court is strictly limited. When a marriage or a relationship breaks down, often the main problems are financial and the maintenance, and issues in respect of children. The court does not have any jurisdiction over divorce - that is a matter for the County Court or the Family Division of the High Court - and parties in a family dispute may choose the level of court in which they wish to commence proceedings. All care proceedings in respect of children, that is to say proceedings instituted by a local authority, commence in the Family Proceedings Court and, where appropriate, for example lengthy proceedings or proceedings which are of great complexity, the justices' clerk may direct that those matters should be completed in the County Court or the Family Division and the cases will be formally transferred to the appropriate court.

Persons who may be present in court

The following are the persons who are allowed to be present during proceedings in court:

(1) Officers of the court.

(2) The parties to the case which is before the court, their legal representatives, witnesses and other persons directly concerned with the case.

(3) *Bona fide* members of the press and media.

(4) Any other persons permitted to be present by the court.

Restrictions on reporting

The only matters which the press may report are:

(1) The names, addresses and occupations of the parties and any witnesses.

(2) The grounds of the application before the court, defences and any counter claims in respect of which evidence has been given.

(3) Any submissions on points of law and the magistrates' decisions in respect of them.

(4) The decision of the court and any comments of the magistrates on their decision.

Welfare of the child

Statute provides that, where the court is called on to determine any questions in respect of:

(a) the bringing up of a child; or

(b) the administration of a child's property or the application of any income arising from it,

the welfare of the child is the paramount consideration. In that respect, the court is required to have regard to the general principle that any delay in determining that paramount consideration is likely to prejudice the child's welfare.

Statute further provides a "welfare checklist" of factors to which the court must have regard in prescribed applications affecting children and their welfare and provides that no order shall be made unless it is in the child's best interests to make an order.

Parental responsibility

Parental responsibility is defined to mean "all the rights, duties, powers, responsibilities which by law a parent has in relation to the child and its property". Quite often, disputes between the parents of a child centre on where a child should live and with whom he should have contact. As parents have responsibilities in such matters, the court will be called on to decide who has legal parental responsibility for a child.

Orders in respect of children

The court has power to make the following orders:

Residence order

This order specifies the person(s) with whom the child shall live.

Contact order

This requires the person with whom the child lives to allow the child to have contact with any other named person. Contact can include visits or staying with other people.

Specific issue order

This order directs what shall be done to determine a specific issue in respect of any aspect of parental responsibility.

Prohibited steps order

This order specifies any matters of parental responsibility that must not be taken without the court's permission.

These orders can only be made in respect of children up to the age of 16 years but, where there are exceptional circumstances which would justify an extension beyond that age, the order may be extended.

Public law proceedings (care proceedings)

Where a child:

(a) is suffering, or is likely to suffer, significant harm; and

(b) that harm, or the likelihood of it, is attributable to:

(i) the care given to the child, or likely to be given if an order were not made, not being what it would be reasonable to expect a parent to give him; or

(ii) the child's being beyond parental control,

the court may, on the application of a local authority, make an order in respect of the child where the court considers that an order would be better for the welfare of the child than no order at all. The orders that may be made are a care order or a supervision order.

Care order

This order designates a local authority to have formal parental responsibility for a child. The parent(s) of the child will still retain parental responsibility but the local authority will determine to what extent, if any, they may exercise it.

Supervision order

This order places a child under the supervision of a social worker or a probation officer as specified by the court. It may be made for a period of one year and, upon application being made, the court may extend it up to a maximum of three years. The function of the supervisor is to advise, assist and befriend the child. Various requirements may be included in the order, such as a requirement of intermediate treatment which requires the child to comply with matters specified by the supervisor in respect of matters such as residence, taking part in specified activities on specified occasions, mental or medical treatment.

The court has power to make interim care or supervision orders.

Private law proceedings

The court has power, on the application of a spouse to a marriage, to order payment of maintenance to the other spouse and/or any child of the family. The order may be made following a finding that a spouse has:

(a) failed to provide reasonable contribution for the other spouse;

(b) failed to provide or make a proper contribution towards reasonable maintenance for any child of the family;

(c) behaved in such a way that the other spouse cannot reasonably be expected to live with him or her; or

(d) deserted the other spouse.

Only the parties to a marriage can apply for maintenance under this provision and it will be for the magistrates to decide, if any of the above grounds are made out, what maintenance should be paid and whether or not a lump sum (maximum £1,000) payment should be ordered.

When deciding on what maintenance should be ordered, the court must have regard to a statutory list of criteria, both for a spouse and for any child of the family. A "child of the family" refers to the natural child of the husband and to a child who is not the child of both parties but who has been treated in every way as a natural child of both.

Agreed orders

If the parties to a marriage have agreed that one should pay maintenance to the other, they may ask the court to make an order in the terms they have agreed without the necessity of proving any of the grounds above. There is no limit on a lump sum payment under this provision but, before making the agreed order, the court must be satisfied:

(a) that one spouse has agreed to make the financial provisions on which an agreed order is sought; and

(b) that there is no reason to think that the order would be contrary to the interests of justice; and

(c) where there is financial provision for any child, that the order would either provide or make a proper contribution towards the financial needs of the child.

Where the parties to a marriage have lived apart for a continuous period of three months, neither having deserted the other, the court may make an order for maintenance even though the grounds as stated above do not exist and neither is there an agreement about any financial provision. The spouse who applies for this order must specify the aggregate of any voluntary payments made for the maintenance of the other spouse and any children in the three month period before making an application for an order. That figure is then the limit that the court may order, provided the figure does not exceed the aggregate figure stated in the application. Lump sums cannot be included in such an order.

Domestic violence

An "associated person" who has suffered violence or serious behaviour to the extent that a Family Proceedings Court should intervene may apply to the court for a non-molestation order. An associated person is:

(1) A spouse, divorcee, cohabitant and former cohabitant; other relatives who live or have lived in the same household; persons who have agreed to marry one another.

(2) In relation to children, parents both natural and adoptive and those with parental responsibility.

(3) An authorised third party.

(4) A child under 16 with leave of the High Court.

(5) The court of its own volition when dealing with a family proceedings application.

When considering whether a non-molestation order should or should not be granted, the court must have regard to all the circumstances, including the need to secure the health, safety and well being of:

(a) the applicant;

(b) the person for whose benefit the order is made; and

(c) in the court's discretion, any relevant child and any child who is living with or ought reasonably to be expected to live with either party and any child who is subject to adoption proceedings or proceedings under the Children Act 1989.

Terms of non-molestation order

The court may order that the respondent shall not molest any named associated persons and any relevant children.

The order may be for a limited period or until further order. If it is made during the course of other family proceedings, it will cease to have effect if those proceedings are dismissed or withdrawn.

In exceptional circumstances, the order may be made by a single magistrate and in the respondent's absence (an "ex parte" order). In prescribed circumstances, a power of arrest may be attached to it, if the respondent has used or threatened to use violence against the applicant or a relevant child and where they are at risk of significant harm from the respondent if the power of arrest is not attached.

When an ex parte order has been made, a full hearing should be arranged as soon as possible for the respondent to make representations.

When a full order has been made, both parties having had notice of the hearing of the application, the court, being satisfied that the respondent has used or threatened to use violence against the applicant or a relevant child, must add a power of arrest unless it is satisfied that they would be adequately protected without that power. A power of arrest enables a police officer to arrest a person whom he has reasonable course to suspect has breached the order. If a power of arrest has not been attached and a breach of the order occurs, the applicant may give evidence before the court of the breach and the court, if satisfied that there are reasonable grounds to do so, may issue a warrant for the arrest of the applicant.

Penalty for breach of an order

If the respondent admits to breaching the order or it is proved on the balance of probabilities that he has done so, the court may order him to:

(a) pay a sum not exceeding £50 for every day he is in breach, up to £1,000; or

(b) pay a sum not exceeding £5,000; or

(c) be committed to custody for a period not exceeding two months or until he has remedied his default in a shorter period.

The committal order is immediate but may be suspended upon a condition of obedience to the order.

The court has power to make other orders for the protection of children, for example an assessment order where on the application of a local authority or the NSPCC the court is satisfied that the applicant has reasonable cause to believe that the child is suffering, or is likely to suffer, significant harm and an assessment is needed for that purpose.

In an emergency situation, the court has power to make an emergency protection order on the application of any person when it is satisfied that there is reasonable cause to believe that the child is likely to suffer significant harm if he is not removed to accommodation provided by the applicant, or on the application of a local authority where enquiries are being made because of the local authority's suspicion that the child is suffering or is likely to suffer significant harm and those enquiries are being frustrated by an unreasonable refusal of access to the child and that access is required as a matter of urgency. The NSPCC may also make an application for the order if it has reasonable cause to suspect that the child is suffering or is likely to suffer significant harm and enquiries as to the child's welfare are being similarly frustrated. The order authorises the removal of the child to the applicant's accommodation and his detention there and gives parental responsibility to the applicant which may only be exercised to the extent reasonably required to safeguard or promote the child's welfare.

An emergency protection order has effect for a period not exceeding eight days and can be extended once for up to a further seven days.

The child, his parents or anyone having parental responsibility, or anyone with whom the child was living before the emergency protection order was made, may apply to the court after the expiration of 72 hours from the time the order was made to have the order discharged, unless they were present at court when the order was made.

Chapter 19

MISCELLANEOUS MATTERS

Written plea of guilty

Where a summons has been issued against a defendant in respect of an alleged summary offence and that offence is either not punishable by imprisonment or is punishable by not more than three months' imprisonment and:

(a) a notice of the effect of the court proceedings; and

(b) a concise statement of facts; and

(c) a notice that the defendant can complete about the facts of the case and any personal history and mitigation

are served on the defendant, he may if he so wishes, plead guilty to the offence in writing without the necessity of appearing before the court.

This written plea of guilty system is widely used, particularly in minor road traffic offences, television licence and vehicle excise licence evasion.

Re-opening cases

The Magiatrates' Court has power to re-open a case to vary or rescind a sentence that has been passed on a defendant, or vary or rescind any order it has made. The power can be exercised if it is in the interests of justice to do so. There is no time limit on the exercise of this power and it may be exercised by a Bench which need not be composed of the magistrates who originally dealt with the case. The court may rescind a conviction and order that the case be re-tried.

This power applies to cases dealt with in the particular Magistrates' Court. It cannot be applied to any case dealt with by a Magistrates' Court in another court area, nor to cases dealt with in the Crown Court or High Court.

Anonymity of magistrates

When magistrates sit in court, they are not allowed to withhold their names from the public, the parties to the proceedings, their legal representatives, the press who are present in court to report the proceedings or any enquirer acting in good faith.

Handcuffing of defendant

It is entirely for the magistrates to decide whether any defendant is brought before the court in handcuffs, provided the prosecutor can show that there are reasonable grounds for apprehending that the defendant will be violent or will try to escape.

Bind over

The court has power to "bind over" any person before the court whose conduct does not constitute an offence but gives the court concern as to his future behaviour in the sense that unless there is a bind over there is a risk of a breach of the peace.

The bind over is an order on a person to keep the peace for a period specified by the court (commonly for a period of 12 months) in a sum of money specified by the court (the "recognisance") which that person will be called on to forfeit if he breaches the terms of the court's order. A bind over is not a sentence of the court but in the case of a defendant it may, in appropriate circumstances, be an order ancillary to sentence. In addition to recognisance of the person to be bound over, the court may require a surety or sureties to enter into a recognisance for the purpose of ensuring that the person bound over keeps the peace.

Forfeiture

The court has a general power of forfeiture in addition to any powers of forfeiture provided by various statutes. Generally, the court has power to deprive a defendant of his rights in property when he has been convicted of an offence if the court is satisfied that the property:

(a) has been lawfully seized from him; or

(b) was under his control or in his possession when apprehended for the offence or when a summons was served on him, and

(i) the property has been used for the purpose of committing or facilitating an offence; or

(ii) was intended for use by him for that purpose.

A similar power exists when the offence consists of unlawful possession of property.

When considering an order, the court must have regard to the value of the property and the likely financial and other effects on the defendant.

The power applies to all offences but does not extend to depriving a defendant of his right in *real* property.

Disobedience of court orders

A person who disobeys a court order other than an order for a payment of money may be ordered to pay either a sum not exceeding £50 for every day in which he is in default or a sum not exceeding £5,000, or may be committed to custody either until he has remedied his default or for a period not exceeding two months.

Custody time limits

Time limits exist with respect to specified preliminary stages of criminal proceedings for an offence as to the maximum period that is allowed to complete that stage and during which, while that stage is being completed, the defendant may be remanded in custody. These custody time limits may be extended by the court, for good and sufficient reasons as specified in the relevant statutory provisions, on the application of the prosecution.

Where a time limit expires before the completion of the particular stage of the proceedings, and the prosecutor has failed to obtain an extension of time, the magistrates have no power to extend the time limit and the defendant must then be granted bail.

Spent convictions

Where a person has been convicted of an offence and certain conditions are satisfied, after a specified statutory rehabilitation period has expired he is to be treated as a "rehabilitated person" in respect of that conviction and the conviction is to be treated as "spent". That person is then to be treated for all purposes as though he was not convicted, charged with, prosecuted or sentenced in respect of that offence.

This provision does *not* apply to evidence given in criminal proceedings and, in particular, a defendant's antecedents provided for the court after conviction should contain *all* convictions. However, no person in court should refer to a spent conviction without the authority of the magistrates. Authority should not be given unless the interests of justice so require it. In passing sentence, the magistrates should not refer to a spent conviction unless it is necessary to do so for the purpose of explaining the sentence that is passed.

Misbehaviour in court

Where any person insults the magistrate(s), a witness, an officer of the court or any advocate having business before the court, during the sitting or attendance in court or in going to or returning from the court, or wilfully interrupts the proceedings in court or otherwise misbehaves, the court may order that person to be taken into custody. The time in custody will be until the rising of the court or, if the court thinks fit, for a specified period not exceeding one month. The court also has power, in addition to or instead of custody, to impose a fine not exceeding £2,500.

Prohibition on publication

Where it appears necessary for avoiding a substantial risk of prejudice to the administration of justice in proceedings held in public, the court may order that the publication of any report of those proceedings or any part of them be postponed for such period as it thinks necessary for the purpose.

Where a juvenile is a defendant, a witness or a victim in criminal proceedings in the Magistrates' Court, the magistrates may direct that any press, radio or television report of the proceedings must not reveal the name, address, school or identity of the juvenile concerned.

POSTSCRIPT - REVIEW OF CRIMINAL COURTS

As this book went to print, Lord Justice Auld, who had been commissioned by the Lord Chancellor to conduct a review of the criminal courts in England and Wales, published his report. The primary suggestion in the report is that the criminal law should be codified and that there should be codes of offences, procedure, evidence and sentencing.

The report recommends that the Crown Court and the Magistrates' Court should be replaced by a unified Criminal Court consisting of three divisions:

(1) The Crown Division.

(2) The District Division.

(3) The Magistrates' Division.

Crown Division

It is envisaged that this Division would be constituted as the present Crown Court, to exercise jurisdiction over all indictable only offences and the more serious either-way offences.

District Division

This Division would be constituted by a judge, normally a District Judge or a Recorder and at least two magistrates. Its jurisdiction would be a mid-range of either-way offences of sufficient seriousness to merit up to two years' custody.

Magistrates' Division

This Division would be constituted by a District Judge or magistrates as the Magistrates' Courts are now. Their jurisdiction would be over all summary offences and less serious either-way offences. The suggestion is that the Magistrates' Division would allocate all either-way offences according to their seriousness and the circumstances of the defendant, looking at the possible outcome of the case at its worst from the point of view of the defendant, bearing in mind the jurisdiction of each Division. In the event of a dispute as to which court would try a case, a District Judge would determine that matter after hearing representations from the prosecution and the defence. The defendant would no longer have a right of election to be tried in any of the Divisions.

Justices' clerks and legal advisers would continue to be responsible for the legal advice provided to magistrates.

The magistrates

Magistrates and District Judges should continue to exercise their summary jurisdiction and the criminal work would continue to be allocated between them much as at present.

In the District Division, the magistrates would sit with District Judges exercising the higher jurisdiction.

The Report goes on to suggest that steps should be taken to provide benches of magistrates which would more broadly reflect the communities they serve, and that the training of magistrates should be strengthened, with the Judicial Studies Board being responsible, and adequately resourced, for devising and securing the content and manner of the training.

A further suggestion is that committal for trial and for sentence by the Magistrates' Division in either-way cases should be abolished: matters too serious for the Magistrates' Division would go direct either to the District Division or Crown Division depending on their seriousness. Pending that procedure, either-way offences should be sent to the Crown Court in the same manner as indictable-only offences.

There would be three main exceptions to trial by jury. First, defendants in the Crown and District Divisions should be entitled with the court's consent to opt for trial by judge alone. Second, in serious and complex fraud cases, the trial judge should have the power to direct trial by himself and two lay members drawn from a panel established by the Lord Chancellor for the purpose but, if the defendant requests it, trial may be by judge alone. Third, a Youth Court, constituted by a judge of an appropriate level and at least two experienced youth panel magistrates, should be given jurisdiction to hear all grave cases against young defendants unless the alleged offences are inseparably linked to those against an adult.

Decriminalisation and alternatives to conventional trial

The report proposes a greater use of a system of fixed penalty notices subject to a right of challenge in court for television licence evasion and the existing provisions for road traffic offences.

The trial: procedures and evidence

In trials by judge and magistrates in the District Division, it is suggested that the judge should be the sole judge of law but the judge and magistrates should together be the judges of fact, each having an equal vote. The judge would rule on matters of law, procedure and admissibility of evidence in the absence of the magistrates where it would be potentially unfair to the defendant to do so in their presence. The judge should not sum up the case to the magistrates but should retire with them to consider the court's decision, which he would give publicly together with the reasons for that decision. The judge should be solely responsible for sentence.

Several matters within the law of evidence are considered to be in need of a comprehensive review as are the ways in which the procedures and facilities of the courts should or could be modernised to better serve the public.

Appeals

The suggestion is that there should be a single line of appeal from the Magistrates' Division and above to the Court of Appeal in all criminal matters, which would mean the abolition of appeal from Magistrates' Courts to the Crown Court and its replacement by an appeal to the Crown Division constituted by a judge alone.

Report summary

A summary of the report can be found on the internet at http://www.criminal-courts-review.org.uk/summary.htm

INDEX

A

B

D

E

H

I

J

L

T

U

V

W

Y